CONTENT CREATORS ARE FULL OF SH*T

How To Be A Winning Content Marketer (and How Not To)

Josh Barney

ISBN: 9798629526575

Book design by: Ivan Kurylenko (hortasar covers)

CONTENTS

Egotistical, Miserly Bastard

INTRODUCTION

4.54 billion people were active internet users in January 2020[1]. That's the equivalent of 13x the United States' population or 67x of the UK's[2] (and approximately 58% of the world's population).

These stats are growing year on year.

Content is the driving force behind these huge numbers and the success of our digital world. Without content and the creators who publish it, we'd have very little reason to open our mobile apps, key in our computer passwords or even turn on the television.

But there's a problem: anybody can publish anything online (including me).

With such a huge number of people going online and few checks or measures on the content that's published there, we've created a perfect storm. An age where content creators can dictate our learning, the information we consume, the news, our opinions on the world, our self-respect, mental health, confidence and so much more.

If you're thinking about entering the digital world as an influencer, marketer, creator or business owner, don't do anything until you've read this.

VERY IMPORTANT: Follow me on Twitter: *@joshbarney-blog,* Facebook: *@joshbarneyb* and subscribe on my website for exclusive FREE access to my upcoming work here: *www.joshbarney.blog/newsletter*

As you'll find out, I am insanely impatient and try to avoid fluff of all kinds (he says at the same time as writing a fluffy sentence)...

...let's stop wasting our time and get into this thing...

'In a time of deceit, telling the truth is a revolutionary act.'

-GEORGE ORWELL

1. CONTENT CREATORS ARE FULL OF SH⋆T

Imagine earning $10-15k just for publishing a 'sponsored' post on social media, as well as making more than $2k per hour for playing your favourite computer game.

Imagine having more than 1.3 million YouTube subscribers, 500,000 Instagram followers and 370,000 Twitter followers.

Imagine (on top of all of that) that you're a professional model with a host of famous friends, and you've not even had your 30th birthday yet.

Sounds good, right?

This was the reality for a well-known content creator. He had what so many people want - an audience, fame, earning power, the freedom to do whatever he wanted and earn 'easy' money while doing it, a life that appeared fun and amazing in comparison to most of yours.

And yet, in June 2019, his backpack, wallet, phone and a change of clothes were found on the pedestrian walkway of a well-known American bridge. His body was hauled from the river five days later.

This social media star had, to the shock of his entire community, committed suicide.

That's part of the reason that I'm awake and writing this for you. It's 5am on a Tuesday morning in a bleak English December.

To me, this feels like a purpose, like I have a responsibility to cut through the noise and tell you the truth. You need to know that your life isn't as shit and boring as social media makes you think it is.

I'm not here to fix something, nor am I going to preach or lecture you on the ways of the world or give you any life-directing bullshit. I'm writing this to expose the problem, because those responsible are a lot like me.

What you're about to read is the whole truth about a profession that calls themselves 'content creators'.

BTW: If you have picked this book up because you're thinking about moving into content (or content marketing) don't start anything until you've finished reading this.

But before we really get into it and I start kicking the hell out of everyone in my industry, I want you all to know that I don't hate my job. It's quite the opposite, I was born to do this stuff.

If you're passionate about making stuff, like to read, possess a imagination and more than anything, hate losing, you'll fit right into the content creation world. Come join the party. You won't dislike content marketing (or creation), in fact you'll probably adore it.

However, there's a problem with the profession that I love: lies - a hell of a lot of them.

I've read, watched and heard a ton of stuff about people like me, and I'll be straight with you, most of it is bullshit.

Content creators (and marketers) spend a large chunk of their time creating content about how they create content. In layman's terms, they're constantly telling the world how they do their job successfully and why they're so good at it. In any other profession that wouldn't cause a problem, but in the world that I'm from, there's a complication with this:

Content creators are full of shit.

I go through the same processes, face the same problems, revel in the same victories and some of the time, I too, am also full of shit.

I understand why it happens and in 99% of cases, I can actually see why content creators get worse.

Anybody who enters this industry is in danger of becoming completely full of shit, but it's not a creator's fault and in the rest of this book I'm going to show you why, explain how you can avoid it and teach you how to be a winning creator for years to come.

2. THIS WILL BE BUMPY

If that first section took you by surprise and you're already thinking *'what the F is a content creator anyway?'* this is where I drag you out from that rock you've been hiding under.

Content is today's buzz word in social media and marketing. It refers to anything that takes up space online - be it social media posts, writing, videos, photos, audio files, interactive elements - it's all content. I could close my eyes, hit a bunch of keys, land on a website and call it content.

If you want my honest opinion, it's a term that was probably coined by somebody who wanted to make more money online and so claimed to be an expert in this new thing called 'content'.

BTW: It's easier to monetise something when it has a 'label'.

Content creators (or marketers) are people who have the aim of growing their digital presence (or that of a brand they represent) by creating and publishing their own work (aka content) on the internet. These include, but are not limited to:

- Marketers
- Designers
- Photographers
- Writers
- Videographers
- Cameramen
- Coders
- Journalists
- 'Creatives' (I hate that word btw)
- Podcast hosts
- Presenters
- Chefs
- Speakers
- Researchers
- Online Businesses
- Models
- Actors
- Dancers
- Singers
- Pet owners
- Artists

(I could go on all day, but hopefully this list gives you the idea)

Some content creators focus mainly on their own websites (like a blogger), some only use social media to grow their presence, others post solely on content sharing websites (like digital magazines) and others, like me, create and share content absolutely everywhere to grow and develop an audience as fast and as big as possible.

The world is full of content creators. The vast majority are unknowing of their amateur status, but the few who refer to themselves as a 'content creator' (aka influencer, social media marketer, blogger etc) understand the power of content and what it means in today's world.

Content drives everything that is valuable online.

You'll come to learn more about the value of content as you make your way through this book, but for now, to truly understand why it's so important, I want you to think about the websites (or internet-based apps) that you visit every single day. If you're struggling, here are some of the most popular in the UK (at the time of writing): Google, Facebook, YouTube, Instagram, Twitter, Wikipedia, Spotify, BBC, Netflix, Amazon, TikTok, Yahoo, LinkedIn, IMDB, TripAdvisor.

When you have a few in mind (5 is more than enough), think about the reason that you visit that website. Is it because you want to see what your friends are up to? Find an answer? Read the latest news? Discover some trending topics or fashions? Kill some time? Be entertained? Be educated? Watch a video? Read something? Listen to music?

The answer, in more than 90% of circumstances, is always content.

Many of the world's top websites (and most valuable brands) do nothing more than give us a platform to share content with each other (think Google, Facebook, YouTube, Instagram, Twitter, TikTok, LinkedIn, TripAdvisor). And the others use their platform to share their own content (think BBC, Wikipedia, Netflix).

Even brands that sell online (like Amazon) have to create content in their ads (e.g. imagery, video, written copy, music) and then post these ads in places where there are people. In other words, they create paid content (ads), and share it in places that other people are creating content (e.g. social media, search engines).

Where there's content, there are people. And where there are people, there's money.

Think of it like this, have you ever followed a profile who didn't post anything online? Or repeatedly visited a completely blank, unchanging website? Or seen a successful social network where nobody posted anything?

Content gives you a reason to go online, to follow others, visit websites and buy from brands.

Content gets people's undivided attention. And the more attention a creator has, the more they're able to earn.

The seemingly complicated world of a content creator can be broken into 3 simple steps:

Content -> Attention -> Money

The problem is that where there's money, people tend to fuck up, screw each other over, make mistakes, cheat, steal, lie, beg and bullshit. In the case of content creators (and marketers) the first two steps in their earning process are steeped in these issues (content and attention).

I'm going to show you where and how they do this, as well as sharing a few of my favourite stories, some of the challenges I've faced in my career and a ton of truths about content.

Strap yourself in. This will be bumpy.

3. I WON'T APOLOGISE FOR THE SHORT CHAPTERS

A lot of the chapters, paragraphs and sentences in this book will be short and I won't apologise for them. I do it for a reason.

Long copy is great, but I always preferred shorter chunks and even though you might deny it and tell your friends that you think *War and Peace* is a much more enjoyable read than this, I know deep down that the majority of you prefer bitesize too.

Creators are shaped by their environment and that, of course, is you.

It doesn't matter if you're an artist, videographer, writer, presenter, designer or ideas man, you don't have a chance if you don't adapt to your audience.

A creator is dead in the water if they don't understand who they're creating for.

That sentence is important (that's why I made it stand out from the rest). Admittedly, it's pretty obvious, (this is only chapter 3, give me a break) but it's worth holding on to and never losing sight of.

The landscape has changed and continues to, every day. This means that there is no 'typical' route, nor is there a distinct blueprint that will lead a content creator to a quick win.

The key to success is being creative, but most of the time that doesn't mean being creative in a 'I'm-adding-to-the-world, I'm-a-great-person' kind of way. It means getting creative in a 'I'm-a-bit-of-a-bastard-here's-my-evil-laugh' kind of way. This requires getting your hands dirty and often times, sacrificing the quality of your work.

To highlight this point and really help you to understand, drink in the following study:

According to the *Statistic Brain Research Institute*, the average human attention span has dropped from approximately 12 seconds in the year 2000, to just 8.25 seconds in 2015[3].

To put this into perspective for you, a goldfish has an attention span of 9 seconds.

The study shows that in just 15 years, the human brain has lost 31.25% of its attention holding abilities (and I'm writing this in 2020! It must be worse now!) What we're undergoing is a psychological devolution and it's all due to technological advances.

Think about the invention of smart phones, super-portable music, the internet, social media and ask yourself, what do they give us when we've got nothing to do?

These advancements in technology provide us with answers, education, entertainment and connection, without us having to do anything. We can discover any answer in the click of a few buttons.

This is amazing when it's used correctly but most of us aren't able to apply the tech as it was intended, and that's had a startling effect on our ability to focus, our attention spans and has thrust content creators into a vicious circle of attention grabbing strategies.

A great example of this is fake news. In 2016, a news company declared that Pope Francis was endorsing Donald Trump's bid for presidency. This article had 960,000+ engagements on Facebook[4] (social media engagements refer to likes, comments and shares, NOT clicks) and was widely believed until being uncovered as fake.

People have never wanted the quick fix, the startling, the amazing, the weird and the whacky in such a massive supply more than they have now, and this has allowed fake news, as crazy as the Pope endorsing Donald Trump, to become believable and spiral out of control.

But what does this all mean for a content creator?

War!

A creator's work is futile if nobody notices it.

A short attention span means lack of focus, it means skipping from place to place without taking anything in, it means scrolling through social media newsfeeds at 100 mph, it means consuming a few seconds of video before abandoning. It means a kick in the gut of all things a creator holds dear.

So much of a creator's effort must go into their opening

gambit and then be followed by constant prompts for their audience to stay tuned in that it punishes quality.

It means, that even though this has always been the way I've written, there's no point in adapting my style. I have to stay punchy, otherwise I'll drown in a sea of ignorance.

If my content doesn't bash you in the teeth every few paragraphs (online), you'll abandon it and go elsewhere, and that sucks.

Create content that appeals to goldfish.

A content creator's style has been forced to change. We must continuously remind our audience that our content is worth another 8 seconds. They've made us this way, and if it's our only hope of survival, we'll do it.

4. YOU CAN'T BE IGNORED

I've always written small, so the whole online content creator thing was an easy step for me.

To get where I am now and to have achieved the stuff I have, I've still had to adapt my style and kick my own artistic pride when it's been down. Content creators will tell you that's how the game works.

I've literally poured pints of blood onto word docs, donated organs to design and experienced what felt like near-fatal brain traumas over simple headlines, only for them to completely fail...

...and then looked at someone else's profile and witnessed a video called '*Cat Pulls Stupid Face*' gain 500,000 views an hour.

The life of a content creator can be a real bitch sometimes.

As time goes on, we learn how to make things more consumable, more bitesize, better primed for a zombie world with short attention spans. This is great, it's how we survive (and compete with cats) but as we do this, we make things harder for ourselves, because our audiences see how easily consumed our content is and their attention span gets shorter. And so we adapt further, and so their attention decreases.

This is the everyday devolution that's taking place on-line.

Nobody knows this situation more intimately than a content creator. It's a key element of my focus before every blog, social post, image, video or strategy that I lay my hands on.

The key to creating content that holds attention is structure. No matter the medium, whether it's:

- Written
- Video
- Audio
- Imagery
- Live

^^^Those bullet-points are the perfect example^^^

A couple years back I spoke on stage (for the first time) about content creation, marketing and strategy in front of 100(ish) business owners who had all paid £3000 to be there. (*Find me looking terrified on stage on my website www.joshbarney.blog*).

I had no experience in the medium and although I'd planned my talk and slides to give them the most I possible could, it was how I structured my content that made it feel -at times- like the audience weren't all that interested.

This is a biggy:

Always structure your shit so it cannot be ignored.

The content can be amazing, it can keep reeling your

audience back in, it can repeatedly slap them in the face, but if it isn't structured to do the same, it's game over.

The next time I spoke on stage, I kept checking in with the audience, asking them to agree, making more eye-contact, having structured breaks in my content to make sure they were with me. And if you're producing video, written, audio or bulky visual content, you need to do the same.

You might've already noticed some of the structural tricks I adopt to keep people engaged and focussed in my written content.

I use bullet-points, numbered lists, short paragraphs that seem like they're ending like this...

...but then I bring them back to life (after an ellipsis). I love to centralise a big statement and make it italic, I like to put a big bold *BTW* at the start of some lines to jig my audience's focus. And most importantly, I am as straight and direct as possible.

In videos, you might've seen screen wipes, switching angles, fast cuts between scenes, text appear, colours, flashes, images, noises, music, catchphrases, the list goes on - they're all designed to reengage you with their content through structured pokes.

If you're a content creator, you need to figure out how you can structure your red-hot content so it can't be ignored. No matter your medium, there's a way of doing it, I promise.

21

5. I WANT TO REPLACE
YOUR MOTHER

Every 60 seconds, this happens online[5]:

- 4.5 Million YouTube videos are viewed
- 188 million emails are sent
- 41.6 million Messenger and WhatsApp messages are sent
- 390,030 new apps are downloaded
- 694,444 hours are watched on Netflix
- 114,583 new blogs are published on Wordpress

BTW: These numbers are up, year-on-year.

What do you think when you see stats like that?

Be honest, does it impress you? Scare you? Worry you? Make you feel indifferent?

As a content creator, these numbers are terrifying. It's like being the owner of a burger joint, coming in to work one day and seeing a McDonalds, Burger King and Wimpy Burger all open up on your street.

In my world it means competition like nothing else.

But it's not the other content creators that I'm worried about, I can navigate past them (I'll show you how to do this later).

The people who scare me most are your friends and family, who are posting more frequently than ever before.

Think about it like this:

It's quiet at work so you scroll through Instagram. I've literally just published an awesome post (at the perfect time, because I've figured out when you're most likely to visit Insta)- it's eye-catching, valuable and has tons of really interesting stuff inside...

...but most of the time you'll never see it and even if you do, you won't view it with the same energy.

Instagram is owned by Facebook and they're clever guys. They know, by your behaviour on their app, who your close connections are and therefore, in what order they should rank posts on the newsfeed.

BTW: More personally appealing content like photos of friends and family, will keep you coming back to social networks like Instagram, which means more money for them in advertising revenue.

So, even though I've published something awesome, (since you were last online) your cousin Sally-Jane has posted a photo with her 6-month-old baby. She's sitting on a swing with little baby Riley in her arms, and they've managed to catch a moment where the baby is (kinda) smiling and it just looks so adorable that you can't help but like and comment on it - the same as everybody else in your family.

And by the time you've finished pressing the love-heart emoji 3 times, your Instagram time is over, focus is lost and you remember that work report needs to be finished in the next 20 mins or John in accounts is going to have a hissy-fit.

This is the battle that I'm faced with every day.

Remember this:

> *When you get (really) good at content creating, you stop worrying about other content creators and start thinking about how you can make followers love you more than they love their friends and family.*

I'll be completely honest with you, I hope this book creates an affinity between us. I hope you understand the pains, trials and tribulations of a content creator, I hope that you want to become a creator yourself and more than anything, I hope it makes you love me more than you love your mother...

...so the next time you go online, you see my content first.

OK, that was a bit tongue in cheek, but you get what I mean, right?

Are you starting to understand why the life of a content creator might be slightly twisted yet? Can you see what all that big talk was about in the opening section? Do you really think you've got what it takes?

'We have to continually be jumping off cliffs and developing our wings on the way down'

-KURT VONNEGUT

6. HE THOUGHT IT WAS BIGFOOT'S SKULL, BUT THEN EXPERTS TOLD HIM THIS

This book is only a handful of pages old and you already know:

> A. I'm full of shit (a lot of the time)
> B. I want to replace your mother

These facts aren't anything special. They're the norm in this industry (even though nobody else is brave enough to admit it).

And although they're only the tip of the content creating iceberg that I'm about to expose, you have to admit that they make a compelling and eye-opening beginning (particularly to a marketing book).

Now that I have your attention, it's my job to up the ante, make sure I live up to the initial hype (that I've generated so far) and provide you with the satisfaction your focus deserves.

In the case of this book, I've teed up my content up for success.

This has been easy in comparison to the day-to-day competitiveness of social media, RSS feeds and content distribution hubs that a creator faces.

This is a book. If you bought it, you're probably going to read it. If somebody has recommended it to you, you're almost definitely going to slog it out through the first 50 (or so) pages, even if you don't like it. But if you've just logged onto a social network and you're scrolling through your newsfeed to find something to quench your short attention span, and you see an article, video, image or podcast created by a brand (personal or business), the majority of you will totally disregard it, no matter how much time, effort and strategic thought a content marketer has piled into creating it.

As a result of this, the general public (and internet user) have forced the world's content creators into a myriad of dirty tactics, some that I advocate and others, that completely tar our profession's name (and reputation).

Here's a quotable that sums that up:

If you're going to get results in the content world, sometimes you're going to have to swallow your artistic pride and do things that are purely aimed at getting attention.

I wish it wasn't this way. I believe that content should be a meritocracy, where the best stuff wins every time, but that's not the world we live in.

A lot of the world's top creators produce shit content, but they do it in a way that generates tons of attention.

As a result, every other content creator has had to adapt their game to compete. What we're looking at here is yet another vicious circle that is progressively reducing the amount of time we spend (strategizing and) creating valuable content and shifting this onto the initial hook (or outward badge) of the content.

This means less value, fewer take-aways and mountains of low quality, quickly produced content that is purely click-focussed.

Content like this makes audience's sceptical, forces people to question their trust in brands online and makes the internet a poorer place in general.

In other words, it's total crap.

We can't control the poor-quality work of others, we can only try to raise the standard ourselves, but to have any kind of impact that means playing the same dirty attention tricks as the content cheats.

One of the first things to grab attention online is your content's headline or title.

Instead of simply using the title to summarise the key messages of your content, you must pour a lot of effort into shaping a clickable, attention grabbing headline.

It's bullshit to think that a 30-minute video with TONS of entertainment and educational value might completely flop because the creator only spent 2 minutes writing a headline, but it's the truth.

Crazy headlines are not a new thing. It's been a massive part of the media industry for as long as news has been published. Do you remember any of these:

- FREDDIE STARR ATE MY HAMSTER, The Sun, 1986 (Unsubstantiated lies)
- WEREWOLF SEIZED IN SOUTHEND, The Sun, 1987 (An unstable man handed himself into a police station claiming to be a werewolf)
- DEWEY DEFEATS TRUMAN, Chicago Tribune, 1948 (Harry Truman actually won the U.S presidential election, even though the Chicago tribune claimed to know the results before anybody else and got it completely wrong)

The important thing to remember is that all those headlines were created by journalists (effectively the main content creators of their time) in an attempt to beat their direct rivals to the newspaper sale. It was newspaper vs newspaper, editor vs editor, journalist vs journalist.

These are headlines created by professionals in a warring industry, desperately trying to convert shelf-browsers, passers-by and window shoppers into buyers.

These headlines sound bad, but they have nothing on the content wars of today. The internet is a place where anyone can create content, publish and share it with the world, and they can use any means that they deem necessary to get more people to click on it.

If you factor in the importance of headlines in this farcical digital culture, you end up with click-hungry headlines like this:

1. This Is Why Hong Kong Billionaire is Offering

$180,000,000 To Any Man Willing to Marry His Daughter

2. This Woman Noticed a Baby Dolphin Struggling on the Beach and Did the Most Incredible Thing!

3. Find Out What Prince George Is Called at Preschool

4. He Thought It Was Bigfoot's Skull, But Then Experts Told Him THIS

5. Guess What Happened When This Enormous Pit Bull Was Left To Babysit

BTW: These are all real headlines.

Headlines like this are all over social media, they run as native ads on other websites, they're used in RSS feeds, YouTube, blogging websites, content hubs...you name a place where people are able to post their own content and I guarantee that there are titles like this on there right now.

But, I'm not the kind of guy to leave people hanging and I know that at least one of those headlines has tickled your interest, so here are the news stories (or facts) behind each of those headlines (just to prove how bad the situation has become):

(They're in corresponding order btw)

1. The billionaire's daughter is a lesbian.
2. The woman put the dolphin back in the sea.
3. Prince George is called by his name, George.
4. It was a rock, not bigfoot's skull.
5. The pit bull licked the baby's face and then fell asleep beside it.

When you look back at the original headlines and then to the actual 'content' of the articles, you start to see what a content creator is up against.

None of those 'stories' deserve to be created, published or shared, let alone pushed behind a click-bait headline.

This type of content (that is absolutely everywhere) has made a content creator's task of attracting audiences and then gaining their trust, so damn difficult.

We have to compete with the clickbait-ers to incite curiosity and drive clicks without looking dodgy, being deceitful or pushing the envelope too far. It's a shit-see-saw situation, go too far either way and you're screwed.

OK, I assume that after all that, you'd probably like to know a few clickbait tactics. Here are some simple headline features that guarantee more clicks:

- You: Nothing calls people out more than when you speak to them directly
- Numbers: The bigger and more obscure the better e.g. 345,987
- Dates: Specific months, seasons or years give articles urgency, but they don't age well e.g. June, Summer or 2020
- Curiosity: What kind of intrigue can you create around your topic?
- Questions: People naturally want to find answers that they don't already know. Ask them questions and they'll watch your video, read your article or listen to your podcast.
- Focus on negatives: People are hungrier to click on content about how NOT to do some-

thing, or discover how they're destroying their chances, than how to do things better e.g. The Errors Costing Some Britons £23 Every Week

If you see a headline that features a few of those tactics, you know the creator must be desperate for a visit (or prepared to risk their brand integrity).

Click 'em or flick 'em, but remember that (most of the time) it's not their fault they're headlines are full of shit, it's what they have to do to compete.

7. 'I HAVE NO IDEA'

One of my favourite online stories took place on the website oneredpaperclip.blogspot.com[6].

This free site was created by Canadian blogger, Kyle MacDonald, who invented it with the sole purpose of trading items.

Kyle's website had very little content, but the small amount of text on the homepage was more than enough. It read like this:

This might not surprise you, but below is a picture of a paperclip. It is red.

This red paperclip is currently sitting on my desk next to my computer. I want to trade this paperclip with you for something bigger or better, maybe a pen, a spoon, or perhaps a boot.

If you promise to make the trade I will come and visit you, wherever you are, to trade.

Hope to trade with you soon!

The website gained very little traction early on, but on 14th July 2005, Kyle successfully achieved his first trade, swapping the red paperclip for a novelty pen in the shape of a fish.

This initial trade tipped the balance, giving him three things:

1. Social proof: Somebody had actually taken part in the red paperclip trade, proving that it was real. People are always wary about being 'the first'. When this position is filled it provides others with reassurance and the safety of following.
2. A living, breathing story: After he'd traded his red paperclip, a real story began, and the people following his blog became part of it.
3. Momentum: The first trade got everything rolling. Kyle had found an invaluable commodity that most content creators are never able to achieve.

On the very same day that he traded the red paperclip for a novelty pen, a website visitor from Seattle reached out to take part in Kyle's next trade, offering a hand-sculpted doorknob in exchange for his fish pen.

Within a fortnight Kyle had traded up again, swapping his doorknob for a camping stove.

Over the course of the next year he continued to trade up from his one red paperclip, including items like:

- A snowmobile
- Holiday
- Truck
- An afternoon with Alice Cooper
- A film role

...and 14 exchanges later, Kyle made his final transaction, trading his way all the way up from one red paper-clip to a house.

But not just that, the town (yes, I said town) that traded him the house, also offered him the chance to have (in addition to the house):

- The position of honorary mayor for one day
- A key to the town (I guess this is like a 'key to the city')
- $200 in cash
- A proposal to build the world's largest red paperclip (which they did)
- A local holiday to be celebrated as 'red paper-clip day' on the day he moved in

This is what the internet, an idea and content was able to achieve in just over a year. Look at your desk now, or inside your bag, or at you dressing table, how many houses could you trade-up to in a year?

The blogger (a form of content creator btw) didn't spend any money on driving awareness for his website. All he did was write content about every single trade.

After he'd made his last trade, the Canadian blogger told a BBC interviewer: "A lot of people have been asking how I've stirred up so much publicity around the project, and my simple answer is 'I have no idea'"

There are tons of stories like this - people achieving phe-nomenal things with no resources, little experience and a very limited strategic idea about how they did it.

There are obvious elements of the red paperclip that are known to crush it online. I've already mentioned the story factor and the power of momentum (both of which I'll talk about later). But for now, I want to highlight something that 99.9% of content creators get wrong every single day of their lives:

> *If you want to win big, create stuff that nobody else is brave enough to.*

That's simple, right?

Content styles, topics and ideas tend to fan out around the leader in each industry. For example, freestyle football videos are all recorded in the same kind of format, highly popular fashion blogs all read the same, most business podcasts are recorded in the same boring structure (by people with monotone voices)...

...I could go on all day.

> *Creators copy the leaders in their space because their styles are proven to work, but by replicating somebody else, a creator automatically limits their success.*

When business owners email me about content strategy advice, (quite often) I'll find the content leaders in their space, perform some analysis (with the help of tools) and make free suggestions based on what has worked for them.

I'll hold my hands up now and say that this is lazy, uninspired and for the most part, the actions of a content creating robot.

Of course, it's not always my fault. I get a hell of a lot of emails from people asking for free advice and if I was to spend all my time replying to them in the same way I do for brands that I'm working on, I'd have no time for anything else in my day.

If you are short on ideas, don't know where to begin and truly lack creativity, look at what everyone else is doing and copy them. Try to do what they're doing but do it better.

It's better to do something, than wait forever for an idea.

However, if you have some creativity, passion for your industry, experience, knowledge, skill and people around you to bounce ideas off (not just 'yes men') you have no excuse for copying others. Be brave enough to put thought into your red paperclip.

You're probably onto a winner if your idea ticks these 3 boxes:

1. Nobody else is doing it (or at least committing to it fully)
2. It scares you
3. It will upset or annoy people

I bet there's already something in your mind. Take a moment to flesh out the idea and write it down.

If you look at that idea on paper and it still scares you, it definitely is something worth pursuing.

BTW: This is the formula I used to measure the potential of this book.

8. YOU BECOME A FEEDER

Most creators that I follow as an 'audience member' (or know behind-the-scenes from a content or marketing perspective) don't ever do anything differently from the leading creators in their space. They replicate their style, content topic and mediums.

By copying the ideas of these so-called leaders, the less-established creators effectively lay the foundations of a pyramid. Not only do they show themselves as a 'follower' of somebody else, but because they are replicating the ideas of somebody else, they will never (only in very rare circumstances) be able to create better content than the original creator.

And as a result, this benefits the leaders in their space.

When you copy somebody else's content, you become a feeder for them.

Think about it like this, if you copy somebody else's content ideas and the audience enjoy it so much that they seek out more it, they'll find the content leader with more followers, likes, comments and shares, and most importantly, more authenticity than you and they'll join their flock, not yours. They'll follow them closely, not you. They'll associate your industry with them, not you.

I've actually had a debate about this with a business owner before. When he didn't like the sound of being 'limited', feeding somebody else or being seen as a follower (instead of a leader) he laid this Tony Robbins quote on me:

'If you want to be successful, find someone who has achieved the results you want and copy what they do and you'll achieve the same results.'

It might surprise you to hear that I actually agree with the basic principle of this quote, but it all depends how it's interpreted.

Is Robbins suggesting that to achieve 'the same results', you need to get the same haircut, wear the same clothes, marry the same person, live in an identical house, take the same holidays, say the same things, walk the same way, write the same stuff and present all your ideas and knowledge in the exact same way?

I don't think so.

The idea of copying somebody who is more successful than you is definitely the right thing to do, because all of the most successful people in the world are creating content…

…their OWN content and the core of that content is not copied, it's original.

The industry leaders, top brands and creators of our time make up less than 1% of the people publishing content online. The other 99% copy them, feed them, idolise them. They find something they regard as a 'winning formula' and imitate it to the nth degree.

I know (and have seen first-hand) creators who do nothing but copy their style, presentation method, medium, backgrounds, lighting, wording, grammar, lay-outs and even their content message from others.

They say things like; 'everybody does it like that' or 'it worked for her, it'll work for me.'

To which I say 'bullshit'.

These same people (even though they won't admit it) have had to spend serious cash to get any kind of results on social, that includes hiring people, paying for ads and following their industry leader's advice (which usually ends in them paying for something e.g. content 'hacks', influence, masterminds, meetings, time, advice).

If you were to strip their results back and look at what they would've achieved had they spent £0 on content, it would probably be something close to 0 too.

Money will get you results in content, but it doesn't mean you're any good at it.

There are many people in the upper-echelons of the content industry, (but not the top) who have literally never thought-up, planned or executed an original idea in their life. All they've done is throw money at copied ideas. These same people are the first to teach others how to live their lives, grow their own presence and create content.

Before we move on, I want to highlight a super-famous quote that is much more appropriate to a successful modern-day content creator.

Good artists copy, great artists steal – Pablo Picasso

Copying will limit a content creator to just 'good', but stealing strategies and making them your own, that's how you become 'great'.

Being a content creator (or artist) who copies and limits themselves to good means:

1. Slow organic growth
2. Success limited by the people you copy
3. Having to spend a lot of cash to generate any serious results (in staff, ads and training)

Being a content creator who steals strategies (without copying or imitating) means:

1. Fast growth and real, engaged fans
2. Unlimited success
3. Free exposure from viral-like content

Ask yourself, what do you want - good or great?

9. IF A SHORTCUT WAS A LEGITIMATE ROUTE, IT WOULDN'T BE CALLED A SHORTCUT.

Where there's money, there are sure to be bastards.

I'm going to reel off some terrifying numbers soon, but before we get into all that, we need to discuss fakers a little more.

If you didn't already know, it's possible to buy 'fake followers' on social media platforms like Instagram and Twitter. These 'fakes' can be bought really cheap and make your account look much stronger.

BTW: A fake follower doesn't make your account any more valuable, but it does make your account look more valuable and increase your earning potential to anybody who doesn't realise that they are fake.

Have you ever met a guy with a really expensive, brand new looking car (usually a coupe) that lives with his mum?

Fake followers are the digital world's version of that guy.

They might look good on first appearances, but as soon as you get under the surface, you soon realise that it's all for show.

I don't know how many of you are new to the idea of buying followers, but a quick Google search shows me that right now I can buy 10,000 fake Instagram followers for £65.99.

The price of followers is microscopic in comparison to what the owner of these accounts can earn through 'sponsored posts'.

The difference between a business paying for a sponsored post on an account with 100k followers and 150k followers, could be worth at least $500 (per post[7]), so it's well worth a creator (or influencer's) time to buy fakes.

Previously, there was no way to track fake followers, but software has now been created to audit and analyse any public social profile.

You'd be forgiven for thinking that the only people buying followers were content creators based out of their bedrooms. That's what I thought before the first results of these social audits were released, but now I look at fake followers in the same way as the majority of athletics events, *'Sure, they're all doping, but who's doping the most.'*

To prove this point, here are some of the world's biggest Instagram profiles alongside the percentage of their followers that are fakes (in a 2019 audit)[8]:

BTW: In the case of these celebrities and brands, we can't be sure whether somebody on their team has bought these fake followers, they've done it themselves or the creator of the fake accounts has tested them on profiles with large audiences. All we know is that it proves that you shouldn't believe everything you see on social (particularly when it comes to content and audiences).

- Ellen DeGeneres- 49%
- Taylor Swift- 46%
- Miley Cyrus- 45%
- Katy Perry- 44%
- Drake- 38%
- Kim Kardashian- 44%
- Ronaldinho- 48%
- Jennifer Lopez- 48%
- Kevin Hart- 46%
- Steph Curry- 41%
- Paul Pogba- 40%
- Ed Sheeran- 40%
- Oprah Winfrey- 34%
- Cristiano Ronaldo- 42%

The total of fake followers that follow these accounts (above) verge on the 1 Billion mark, and we're only just getting started[9].

All I've done is pull out some of the most well-known names from the reams and reams of famous profiles involved, and that's without mentioning others like LeBron James, Britney Spears, Eminem and Beyonce (who each have 10m+ fake followers on their Insta accounts[10]).

I'm not going after any of these names, nor am I blaming them for the fakeness that surrounds the numbers on social media (I'm sure they didn't buy followers), but I want you to see it. It's important, particularly for the social sanity and mental wellbeing of a generation that seemingly rely on social media follows and likes for acceptance.

Don't compare your numbers with a celebrity's or 'influencer's' on social media, they're not relevant and most of them are bullshit figures anyway.

Every time a profile on social (especially Instagram) buys followers, they don't just lie to the rest of the world, they also damage a generation who idolise, copy and measure themselves against them.

It's thought that heavy social media usage can more than double the chance of mental health problems in the youth of today (more on mental health in content creation and social media very soon).

My personal opinion is that anybody who buys followers is sad and insecure. If you're thinking about buying a following on social to pretend that you're popular, stop. There's more than enough knowledge in this book for you to grow your audience, and the game's up now, most brands know about this bullshit tactic and are prepared to call you out on it.

If a shortcut was a legitimate route, it wouldn't be called a shortcut.

As well as buying followers, there are other commodities and automation services that act in a similarly disingenuous way on social media, these include:

- Buying likes: As well as buying followers, you can also buy likes from fake accounts. Profiles do this to look more popular (social proof signals), boast about high engagement rates (to brands looking for influential creators) and to have their posts featured more prominently on Explore and Discover pages.
- Follow/Unfollow: When you buy this service, you allow bots to take control of your 'follow' feature. These bots will constantly follow real accounts in the hope that it earns your profile a follow back in return. The bot will then unfollow all the accounts it had followed. It tricks people into reciprocating follows and is very popular.
- Commenting: This service allows bots to take control of your comment feature. It will automatically find new posts tagged with hashtags (that are relevant to your aims) and make generic comments on those posts (usually emojis or random compliments). This gets attention and encourages people to check out your profile.

Many of the 'services' available to content creators use a mixture of these automated processes to mislead prospective followers.

I have seen creators who post content that is supposed to 'help others' use all of these services to build their profiles. It seems ironic that people like this want to lie to others, so they can 'help' them. In fact, it doesn't make any sense at all.

'If you tell the truth, you don't have to remember anything.'

-MARK TWAIN

10. A MILLION DOLLAR STORY

As you make your way through this book, you'll read some of my favourite internet-based stories. As much as I want to open your eyes to the stuff that makes our profession so twisted, I also want to inspire you.

I'm not sure if this tale of internet success has ever been categorised with content, but I'm going to go out on a limb and pull it in.

The idea was conceived by Alex Tew, a student from Wiltshire (that's in South-West England btw) who wanted to earn money online to pay for his university education.

Alex was 21 years old at the time and was concerned that after university he'd be left with a large debt that would take years to repay.

With the investment of just €50, Alex bought a domain name and web-hosting package and went live with his plan on 26th August. 129 days later, on the 1st January, he'd returned $1,037,100 on his initial investment.

The story, much like the red paperclip blog, relied on

the unfolding of a story, an original idea, momentum and social proof.

The website that Alex built was hosted at the address: milliondollarhomepage.com. It made no bold claims, it didn't lie or pretend to be something it wasn't, Alex didn't hide behind a ruse of 'helping people', he made it clear what he wanted: a million-dollar website.

Instead of creating his own content for the website, he made his homepage into a 1000x1000 pixel grid and put each one of these pixels up for sale at the price of $1 per pixel.

If he was able to sell every single pixel on the website it would return (yep, you guess it) $1,000,000.

Anybody that knows anything about tech will tell you that 1 pixel is almost impossible to see on a computer screen with the naked eye. Alex adapted around this, selling 10x10 pixel blocks for $100 a time.

In the first fortnight Alex sold 4,700 pixels to friends and family members, with nothing more than word-of-mouth to market his website.

That's before things took off.

Alex sent out press releases and early in September, one of them was picked up and published by the BBC. This was followed by two articles on the news website 'The Register', and by the end of September (just 6 weeks after its creation) Alex's website had earned him $250,000.

His site continued to grow, increasing in traffic every day, as more and more sites picked up on the story. By the end of October (just 10 weeks after its creation) the million-dollar homepage had sold more than half of its pixels, bringing in $500,000 for the soon-to-be student.

More pixels were sold and at the end of the year, Alex reported that the milliondollarhomepage.com was bringing in 100,000 unique visitors an hour and was ranked as the 127th most visited website in the world by Alexa rankings (a widely trusted traffic analysis tool).

Demand grew to such a level for the last remaining pixels, that instead of selling them for $1 per pixel in a first-come, first-serve basis, Alex placed the final 1,000 on eBay for auction.

After ten days and 99 offers, a bid of $38,100 won the auction (38x the original price) and the journey of the million dollar homepage was complete with every pixel sold, generating $1,037,100 in revenue for Alex.

The website worked because advertisers wanted to be part of Alex's story. They realised that he'd come up with something original, honest and aspirational, and this feeling had tapped into the general public.

This wasn't a celebrity or financially-backed individual, this was a student who wanted to pay his university fees. He was real, so much more so than most of today's content industry.

People will get behind you when you're real. Make your content an extension of yourself.

As a creator, it's crucial that you understand the importance of realness and authenticity. Don't try to be somebody you're not, don't copy others and don't lie to the people who will make or break you (your audience).

Be yourself and be transparent with your objectives. People will support you when you give them reason to.

11. THE LOOK AT MY HOLIDAY AND CRY PACKAGE

In 2018, a website was launched with the slogan:

'Life isn't perfect.
Your profile should be.'

The website, known as *LifeFaker*[12] offered 'packages' for social media posting content. These were aptly named under categories like:

- The Look At My Holiday And Cry Package
- The I Just Happen To Live Here Package
- The I Can Be Arty And Deep Package
- The My Unachievable Body Package
- The I Own All The Things Package
- The I Found Love And Babies Package
- The My Weekend Was Amazing Thanks Package
- The Look What I Had For Lunch Package
- The Yeah My Job Let's Me Travel Package
- The Even My Cat/Dog is Happier Package

The website claimed to be the world's first online faking service, informing prospective customers that 'instead of going through the hassle of living the perfect life, now you can just get the photos.'

The most worrying thing about this website is that I know it will sound appealing to some of you. In fact, I can think of at least 5 people that I know personally who would happily pay a subscription for a *'Life Faker'* account, and I also know a ton of (past and present) peers who would do the same.

Fortunately, the website isn't real. They're as fake as the photos they promise. When you try to buy their service, a full-screen pop-up appears that reads:

'Ever felt the pressure of social media? You're not alone. 62% of people feel inadequate comparing their lives to others'.

The website and idea for *Life Faker* was created by a company called *Sanctus*, a mental health awareness organisation. We'll get to mental health really soon, but first, I want you to understand why I have to talk about the increasingly common topic of faking it in a 'marketing' book.

The reason that *Life Faker* drew so much attention is because it's a service that perfectly sums up the current state of social media and the content creators who excel on there.

We have all been guilty of 'life faking' on social media at some point in our lives - in fact, it's more than likely that your last post is a life faker moment.

If you have an Instagram account, look at your last post: does it truly represent the day, experience and emotions you felt? Do you look how you normally do? Have you used a filter? Is your description a true representative of how you felt?

Please don't think that just because I'm accusing you of faking it, that I'm not guilty of it too. I have felt the pressure to post only the best side of myself, I too have been through photos and found none that I wanted to publish, I have used filters and photo-editing tools, I've cropped, tweaked and trashed anything that didn't fit the 'perfect life' bracket, I've seen others' social content and felt inadequate or inspired to 'top' them, I've uploaded an image, video or comment, only to look at it for five minutes and decide against posting it...

...this is the norm of social media. I have been part of this problem and I'm almost certain that you have too.

Social media sells fakeness as real life.

This problem doesn't just affect personal profiles - brands and businesses have never been under more pressure to show themselves as the 'perfect business' with the 'perfect story' and the 'perfect staff'.

The level of content bullshittery (cool word, right?) on social media is frightening, and as time goes on, it's only going to get worse.

If you've ever visited a social media site, you will have seen the infinity pools, crystal clear seas, immaculately presented vegan meals, clifftop yoga retreats, chiselled six-packs, hourglass figures, glistening hair styles, white bathrobes, tropical sunsets, picturesque hotel rooms, perfectly drawn baths, amazing offices, straight teeth, glowing skin, you will have seen the man standing on stage or sitting behind an over-sized desk, telling you how to live your life and how you can have all the things that he does.

I have news for you, it's all bullshit.

These moments are manufactured. They're put together by professional content creators, who try everything they can to produce the perfect moment(s) in life. And in order for them to do that, they don't just capture one of those moments, they capture 100's, if not 1,000's of them. They stage it over and over again so it looks like they have the 'perfect life'.

These social media content creators are known as 'influencers' or 'personal brands' and they believe themselves to be 'internet famous'.

I don't dislike these people, but I do understand the power that they hold over social and the content that's published there, particularly over amateur content creators (anybody who isn't paid for posting on social).

After a pro publishes a 'perfect life' photo or video, the amateurs follow, like, comment and share their post, making this piece of content appear aspirational (both to them and their followers).

When something becomes aspirational, it is envied, copied and grows into a highly sought-after commodity, encouraging amateurs to feel 'wowed', inadequate or to do everything in their power to achieve similar (if not better) content for their profile.

As the influencers battle each other for attention on the newsfeed, they push each other further and further away from what's deemed safe and achievable.

Many of these social content creators are on a mad mission to get a better snap than their rivals, but with only so much of the world to capture and only so many activities available, some of these creators appear to be losing grip on reality.

It's like two 11-year-old boys trying to impress the prettiest girl in class with dumber and dumber stunts.

In the last month (or so) I've seen two absolutely mental pieces of content on social that have proven how out of control this industry is becoming (especially to younger eyes).

The first is a photo of a travel influencer couple, who I refuse to name because I know that some of you will follow their content (which is the opposite of what I'm trying to achieve with this book).

The pair are on a cliff. The guy is sitting on the very edge and is holding his partner with (almost) outstretched arms, as she dangles in a kind of walking pose in thin air. The cliff is at least a few hundred feet up.

Attached to this photo is the caption: *'The world is waiting for you! Behind the masses of those that wish to watch you lead a quiet and sedentary life is an open, unlined canvas. We urge you to take a chance, to push past barriers of negativity and oppression of self-fulfilment and paint the picture of who you want to be.'*

The couple, who don't seem to understand the damage and potential implications of publishing 'aspirational' photos of themselves hanging off cliffs, are not just showing these sorts of images to their audience, they're goading them to join them (in the description).

They're preaching to others about how to live their lives, in the classic, regurgitated, almost generic social media message 'anything is possible, man', 'our life is perfect, follow us, like our photos and you'll be able to get it too', 'if you don't live like us, you're sedentary and lazy, and uncool.'

The message is trash, let's be clear about that.

However, the vast majority of the damage is done in the photo. In a social content world where influencers are constantly trying to top each other and amateurs are repeatedly attempting to replicate their photos, what's next? What follows this? How will other influencers (both professional and aspirational amateurs) try to top this?

This photo was published to much furore, but it doesn't appear to have affected the couple, in fact, the extra exposure seems to have had the opposite effect. A quick look at their profile and I can see 4 more photos that are similarly dangerous.

Today's influencers are role models, yet nobody holds them accountable for their actions.

I don't think this couple are solely to blame, even though it looks like I'm having a go at them, it's the industry as a whole that has pushed them to this limit. Photos like this are the lengths they've had to go to, to get attention and out-compete their closest rival, and somebody, sooner or later will do the same to them.

And if the cliff example wasn't enough, this next one will definitely make your head spin.

In 2019, a television show aired called *'Chernobyl'*[13]. The show dramatized the nuclear power plant disaster of the same name in 1986.

Naturally, when something like this airs on television, interest grows in the event. This had a startling effect on tourism to the area, particularly the still-dangerous 'Exclusion Zone' which covers approximately 2,600m^2 around the Chernobyl nuclear plant.

Although this area is still considered hazardous (with high levels of radiation) people are allowed to visit if they are accompanied by licensed guides. So, guess who flooded the area as soon as they saw a growing public interest?

Yep, you guessed it, influencers.

If you follow anybody on Instagram (who calls themselves an influencer or content creator) you might have seen some content from the Exclusion Zone, probably with a description that reads something like:

'Life is only lived once. Make the most of it, you never know what tomorrow will bring. RIP Chernobyl #livingmybestlife #youcandoit #throwbackthursday.'

A few stupid and incredibly unthoughtful influencers have come in for criticism for the type of photos they've taken within the exclusion zone.

If looking at a half-naked woman, who is just about wearing a hazmat suit and g-string, in an area where people were killed, contaminated with a slow killing radiation and an entire country (and continent) were devastated, is your kind of thing, you're in luck!

The content creator who posted this photo isn't alone either, there are several others who seem to have forgotten who they might be offending with this type of content (and that there are still people alive whose lives were ruined by this incident).

This is what people have to do to stand out and get attention on social media. A regular post of the Chernobyl Exclusion Zone should be interesting enough, but with the way content creation is going (and the amount of bullshit that's involved in the industry) it's difficult to blame the individual content creators.

12. I AM ONE WITH THE HORIZON

Content has done well for me so far (fingers crossed it continues that way) and last year, I spent an awesome fortnight in Bali, Indonesia.

I go on holiday every year (usually a few times), so what I saw wasn't anything new, but it was the sheer scale of it that took me by surprise.

Bali is undoubtedly an Instagrammer's paradise, but if you're planning to go there, be sure to mentally prepare yourself.

If you want a snap of any of the well-known (and most beautiful) spots on the island, ready yourself for queues. This is normal in a lot of beautiful parts of the world - the problem in Bali wasn't the number of people, it was the way people were taking photos.

These are a few of the names I came up with for the poses I witnessed in Bali:

- *The whimsical*: A playful smile, usually taken with hands raised holding a delicate object (e.g. a flower), whilst looking up and away from the camera lens.

- *The distant rider*: Turn your back to the camera and push out your ass. If you're holding a surfboard, even better! Whatever you do, don't turn around. The back of your head is what people really want to see.
- *The pout and lean*: Bend your back slightly, pout towards the camera and gesture a kiss to your audience.
- *The I am one with the horizon*: Stare so intensely at the horizon that you see yourself on it, playfully dancing on the distant plateau.
- *The sideways awe*: Lay on your side, with your head flat on your arm (which is also lying flat on the ground). Allow strands of your hair to drape over your face, as if you hadn't placed it there on purpose. Roll in the sand for extra effect.
- *The rump's edge*: Sit on the edge of something, a pool, a cliff, a wall, a fountain, it doesn't matter, as long as your legs hang down on the other side and your ass is pumped out in a perfect peach towards the camera. Arch your back and lean away from the lens.

I have stood by and watched people go through all of these poses (and more) whilst waiting to get a simple photograph of a sunrise, horizon or view.

I cannot be completely excused from posing, I took a few photos that I thought would help my life look that little bit better on social media. But, looking back through all my published posts now, my favourite photo of the entire trip didn't even make the cut.

I posted photos of me on picturesque beaches, at the famous Tanah Lot temple, with Monkeys in the jungle, atop Mount Batung and even swimming with turtles, and they're all beautiful shots, but my favourite piece of content from the fortnight is of me on the back of a moped. I'm a bit tipsy, grinning directly into the camera like a Cheshire cat. It's too dark to see much in the background except for a few of the poverty ridden houses (that Bali is full of btw).

Forget every other piece of content from that trip, to me, nothing summed up the holiday better than that shot. I was happy, I was travelling, I was a little drunk and on the back of a moped. It was real. More real and more often than the mountain or the monkeys, more representative of my entire trip than the turtles, more Bali than any of the other photos I had to queue up to take.

Isn't that what content should be about? Isn't this what our social media profiles should really represent?

13. YOU CANNOT MAKE THIS SHIT UP

Is it right for a content creator who wants to help people, promote mental wellness, preach health and stability, and advise others how to get the best from their lives, fake so much of it?

What is even more troubling, is the extent that these people are willing to go to, to fake their lives on social media.

During my (previously mentioned) Bali holiday I saw several promoted tours that were advertised as Instagram Expeditions - promising customers the most photogenic locations, as well as skipping all the queues to the hottest spots.

Content fakery continues to increase in demand, and where there's demand, there's an opportunity to make money.

A little while ago I spoke about the *Life Faker* website, a hoax website set up to raise awareness about mental health and the damage that's being caused by social media.

Whilst *Life Faker* wasn't a legit business, there are other companies that offer serious, paid services that perform exactly the same function.

An example of this is a service called *Fake a Vacation*[14]. For as little as $19.99 (this is their cheapest option btw) you can send this company photos of yourself in your garden, on the toilet, riding your neighbour's dog, pretty much anywhere and they'll crop, edit and paste you into a Las Vegas backdrop. *(I bought this service and posted it on my website: www.joshbarney.blog! Check it out!).*

You cannot make this shit up.

If you're willing to spend a bit more, they'll put you in Hawaii, New York or even Paris! And they don't just send you snaps of you in your dream holiday location, they'll also deliver information about your fake vacation directly to your inbox.

BTW: I'm not going to reveal anymore company names because I don't want to give them any extra exposure. If you really want to fake your life on social media, find them yourself.

What makes things worse, is that several Instagram influencers have actually been caught out faking their own travels.

I've read tons of reports (this year) about content creators mysteriously floating a few inches from the ground (like they've been badly photoshopped and don't match the image perspectives) and heard about travel influencers who have been caught with the exact same clouds following them around all over the world.

But photoshopping isn't all they're doing, there are other ways that Instagram influencers and content creators are faking their perfect lives. Here are some of the most extreme cases:

(I could fill 10 books with the amount of bullshit that content creators spit out on Instagram, but for now, let's call it a day with this short list).

Fake private jets:
If you don't own a private jet, what's the point of being on Instagram? You're a content creator, how could you possibly fly with the riff-raff on a normal aeroplane? There is a way around it, simply build a fake private jet cabin and take snaps there. That's what they did in L.A.[15] and Instagrammers flocked from all over the world to capture photo or video content in the sitcom-like set.

Fake sponsored posts:
Want to be an influencer, but don't have the audience? Fake it until you make it honey. Take photos of some of the biggest brand's products and pretend that they're sponsoring you. This will make you look much more (cough) professional when real businesses are looking for somebody to sponsor.

Fake your Family:
A company in Japan called *Family Romance* have created a service where you can hire actors to pretend to be your girlfriend, neighbour, best-friend, grandma, second cousin[16]...you want a fake friend or family member, you got it. Want a fake baby? These crazy bastards even offer that too! You can even hire a group of actors and pretend you're at parties, events, dance-offs, Instagram tours...

you name the experience and they'll fake it.

Rent it all and pretend it's yours:

Why does everyone on Instagram seem to own a Lamborghini, yet I never see them when I'm out on the road? Does everyone have a spare Lambo in their garage? Why am I the only one who doesn't have one?

Anything can be rented, snapped as content and pretended to be yours. People do it with apartments, cars, clothes, jewellery, helicopters…if you can rent it, content creators will pretend to own it.

These are just some of the ways that Instagram content creators are bullshitting their audience. I understand that people want to look amazing on social and only want the world to see their best side, but at the very least, we expect that to be real, right?

If the best side of you is fake, what does that say about you as a person?

To take a little peek into the potential future of social media, I want you to have a closer look at one of Instagram's hottest influencers right now (at the time of writing).

She's only 19 years old, but she already has over 1.7 million followers.

Her CV shows that she's modelled for brands like Calvin Klein, Supreme, Chanel and Prada, appeared in Vogue, The Guardian, BBC and Buzzfeed.

She's released songs, collaborated with famous musicians, been snapped with tons of other Instagram influencers and celebrities as well as featuring in music videos. The Brazilian-American model has even appeared in magazine ads, whilst hopping between her homes in New York and LA...

...but even though she seemingly has it all, something isn't quite right with this young lady.

At first glance, she looks like a normal model and creator. From certain angles you can see the gap in the centre of her teeth and when the camera's close-up you notice just how many freckles she has. Her eyebrows are bushier than you'd expect from an Instagram model, but they seem to perfectly fit her smooth complexion.

The model in question is known as Lil Miquela and she's not human[18].

The 'virtual influencer', who let me remind you has 1.7 million followers right now (and that number will be higher by the time you read this) is computer generated. She's managed, controlled and owned by a start-up business in L.A.

How long will it be until we can't tell the difference between the real content creators and the controlled (aka the computer generated)?

Lil Miquela is not the only one either. More and more of these computer-generated models are popping up on Instagram, as other companies jostle for a model that they can do absolutely anything with.

If you wanted (and had enough cash to throw at it), you could have shots of Lil Miquela leaning against the ruins of Machu Picchu in Peru and seconds later, see shots of her propping up the Leaning Tower of Pisa in Italy.

You can have her wearing 100 different fashion brand's clothing all at the same time, she can never age, never get pregnant, never put on weight, never get acne, never have a bad hair day, never turn up for work hung-over, never have a sassy tantrum and tell her photographer to 'fuck-off'.

Lil Miquela is a glimpse into the murky content future that could be waiting for us.

If we ever get to a point where the world's most popular social media influencers (and content creators) are virtual, we will be treading on very dangerous ground.

Social media influencers (usually) have large audiences and as the name suggests, huge amounts of influence over their followers. If their every action, attitude and expression is dictated by a business (or group of people), influence can be centralised, controlled and managed by the highest bidder.

Consider for a second, the effect a social media influencer has over their youngest followers, and then consider the messages that the world's biggest brands want to instil in their mindset.

What we're potentially looking at are social media 'influencer' factories, churning out computer generated fake after fake in a profit chasing industry.

For now, keep an eye out for virtual influencers and when you see them, beware of the messages they're sending out. You'll never know who really wanted to send those messages and more worryingly, what they're trying to achieve with them.

14. A HELL OF A LOT OF PAIN

Content creators are full of shit. By now, you should understand why I can make that statement with assured confidence.

There are plenty more reasons, examples and stories of big time content creator bullshittery and trust me, I've saved my absolute favourites until later in the book (for those of you kind enough to stick around), but before we get into all that, I need to explain why so many of these creators get caught up and lost in their own horseshit.

Being a content creator is fucking difficult.

If you're on the outside looking in, and you honestly think that being a content creator looks like a cake walk, you're clueless.

Content creation is tough. Anyone who's experienced the ins and outs of the industry over a prolonged period of time, will understand the pain involved.

To many of these people, particularly those who've entered the industry alone in the hope of emulating the creators they idolise any shortcut means a little less pain.

And when a creator starts out, they'll have to endure a hell of a lot of pain.

'There is nothing to writing. All you do is sit down at a typewriter and bleed.'

-ERNEST HEMINGWAY

15. SHIT BOULDER,
SHIT HILL

The early stages of a content creator's career are hell (for 99.9% of us).

The work can be interesting and there are heaps of new experiences, but on the whole, it's an uncomfortable experience.

There are exceptions who make a fast and meteorically rise to the top, and there are also those who join brands (or teams) that are already established online and from there it's all about optimising and growing further (the easiest of a content creator's tasks).

But for everyone else (the vast majority), it's a very uncomfortable experience. A quick scan through my email contacts reads like a minefield of *content-creators-for-merly-known-as-content-creators* and the same applies to my social media connections too.

The problem for new creators always begins with expectations. Dreams are amazing, aims are even better, but if you really believe something is just going to happen (in an industry like this one) you're doomed for disappointment, heartbreak and failure.

Content creators, marketers and brands quit all the time because their expectations are misaligned.

To demonstrate, let's play a little game. Follow these instructions and see how you get on:

1. *Put your hand out in front of you*

2. *Turn your hand palm up so you can see that there's nothing inside*

3. *Squeeze your hand into a closed fist*

4. *Stare at your hand and believe that there's a delicious walnut inside of it*

5. *Now start to expect that when you open that hand, there really is a walnut inside of it*

6. *Really believe it! This has to work, there must be a walnut in there!*

7. *Open your hand*

Were you one of the lucky few who had a walnut magically appear?

If you weren't, I want you to repeat this exercise 100x and each time you try it, I want your expectations to be higher.

How do you think you'd feel after failing this task 100x? Do you think you'd want to try it another 100x? What do you think would happen to your belief?

Now, let's pretend that I ask you to do this amongst a group of other people and that when they open their hands, some of them have these delicious walnuts magically appear.

Not only do these people clearly demonstrate that it can be done, they also prove that you're pretty shitty. I mean, you tried 100x, you really believed it would happen, you expected results and you didn't achieve anything...

...but they did...

...what does that say about you?

They're magic but you aren't?

This all sounds pretty stupid (I have no idea where this walnut idea came from) but it perfectly explains why so many bloggers, videographers, podcasters, writers, models, photographers, artists, influencers...basically any kind of content creator, give up.

So many talented, brilliant people, who have an amazing set of skills to share with the world throw the towel in before they've achieved anything because the start is so fucking difficult.

Starting out as a content creator is like rolling a shit-boulder up a shit-hill, in shit-shoes, with shit-hands.

This is why so many people see content creators who've made it online (and I mean really made it) and they say to themselves, 'I could do that. They're living the dream life. They've got it easy.'

What I'm getting at here are the computer game reaction video guys, the travel influencers, the repetitive fashion bloggers, the monotonous podcast hosts, the dullard marketing preachers, the angry celebrity gossip girl, the idiot pranksters, the repetitive mindset guys...

...they've made it because they've had more balls than anybody else. They've gone further than people with 10x their talent, they've fought harder and put up with more than most would ever deal with. They've been fucked, came out and gone in again.

So, the next time you see a content creator online (in any form) who looks like they've achieved something (e.g. a large audience, tons of followers, loads of traffic, financial reward from content) and you say to yourself 'I could do that', re-read the next few sections of this book and think again.

16. WHAT AM I DOING TO DESERVE THIS?

When you start a new job, colleagues will show you how to perform the functions of your role (your day-to-day tasks), they'll explain what you should wear, how you should act, where everything is, they'll reveal the company's secrets to success, provide training and then they'll even help you implement it.

Being a content creator is a little bit different.

For starters, you're going to be alone a lot of the time (or at most in a small group). That means no initiations, no walk-throughs, no on-the-job explanations, no training.

If you visit a search engine like Google or YouTube and try to find out how you can start out blogging, podcasting, YouTube-ing, Instagramming, you'll find 1,000's of guides, cheat-sheets, helpful posts and explainers, and many of them will give you a very solid blueprint for success...

...but there are problems with this:

1. Very few of them handle the over-the-top expectations of newly starting out creators

2. They rarely explain how to implement the strategies for success e.g. I might tell you to put 30 hashtags on your Instagram post...but what ones should you use? Where can you find them? On what part of the post should you add them? How can you measure them? How do you actually add these 30 hashtags? What do you do afterwards? Does it matter if you don't do it on every post?

3. There is no guide, article or video that can explain everything you need to know. Most of the things you'll learn will be on the job, particularly as you're creating and publishing.

4. (BONUS) None of them tell you how much bullshit is involved in the life of a content creator

Simply reading a guide and believing that it will work for you is very dangerous.

Remember all those sections that we've just been through - people can fake, lie, cheat, hide and buy their way to success, and then pretend that they have a winning recipe that will work for anybody online.

If you notice anybody who gives themselves one of the following titles, be careful when you see their 'guides':

- Guru
- Ninja
- Hacker

Another reason that these guides are so dangerous is the overwhelming stats and social proof that sit alongside them. For instance, if you watch a video on YouTube about how to become a YouTube star, and that video has 2.3 million views, you automatically believe (consciously or subconsciously) that the tips in that video will help you achieve millions of views too.

Content creation isn't like being a postman.
There is no set route.

The same goes for blogging. I am a blogger and I often share my best advice and strategies for growing a blog, but I am always careful to warn readers about their expectations. If you visit one of my pieces of content and see that it has 1,000's of social shares and is getting tons of traffic, you'll probably believe that by replicating the formula I've laid out, you'll achieve the same pretty quickly, but that just isn't the case (and I make sure my readers know it!).

The same principle applies to Instagram influencers, podcasters, musicians, photographers, or anyone else hoping to become 'internet famous'.

The creators of these 'guides' make everything sound so simple, and there's a good reason for it - it glamorises them. They make their life look easy on purpose, they want to be envied, stand-out, look special and adored, this is all part of the content creator charade.

Guides that show others how to achieve quick results also highlight creators as experts in their industry. This is why so many content creators publish alternative types of content to share advice. This broadens their reach and betters their positioning (in their niche).

For instance, how many Instagram 'influencers' run blogs that share same-same-but-different content? How many bloggers have YouTube channels explaining what they've done to realise their results as a blogger? How many YouTubers promote eBooks that document their path to success?

Whatever way you look at it, these guides and alternative long form content types work out really well for content creators but can have a hugely negative impact on viewers (particularly on their expectations).

I am part of a few different threads and 'creator' groups, and the most common posts in these groups are always from new(ish) creators who aren't getting the results they assumed they would.

It's tough to blame them. They live in a world where the people they're trying to replicate can get 10k new followers, 37k likes, 9k shares and 13k comments just for sneezing. On top of this, barely anyone is trying to reel in their expectations. In fact, most creators actively try to raise them (with their content).

On one of the creator threads (that I'm part of), there is currently a post from a creator who has been publishing new stuff for 2 years. He says that he's *about to give up and call it quits.*

He goes on to say that he *learned from the YouTubers who have been doing this for years.* And that he has done *'EVERYTHING SERIOUSLY like a 1m channel would have.'*

And yet, 23 hours after posting his latest video, it had only received *'17 views'.*

He signs off saying *'What am I doing wrong to deserve this?'*

The entire post is long, angry and clearly very emotional, but how would you feel? He's been trying to become a serious content creator for 2 years, and after all that time and effort, his videos are receiving barely any views or attention.

BTW: His results are on the extremely poor side, but they are still indicative of systemic problems.

I can't vouch for the quality of his content, but even if he is posting crap videos, after 24 months of following the instructions of top YouTubers, you'd expect some sort of traction, wouldn't you?

17. YOU ARE ZERO

I will explain how you can make it as a content creator and I'll show you how to get over the initial ice-cold shock, but before we get onto that, I want to alter your expectations.

If you honestly believe that you can start a new blog, website, YouTube channel, podcast or social media channel and expect people to flock to it, you're greener than an English meadow in spring.

When you start out, nobody is going to give a flying fuck about you.

Why should anybody give a damn about you? What have you proven online that gives you the right to expect people to care? What makes you better than everybody else? What have you learnt from an online guide that's going to help you more than another creator's years of experience?

I know that you're adding hashtags, sharing your stuff on social, following the 'guides' to the letter and trying your best, but you aren't alone - there are millions of other people doing the same thing.

Most fresh-faced content creators seem to forget how many other creators:

- Have something valuable to share
- Are in the exact same position as them
- Have kicked off their content journey a year before them (and although their audiences are tiny, they're still a year ahead)
- That the internet has given a voice to anyone who has something to say

Too many people assume that it's going to be a cakewalk (this is largely the fault of the established content creators) and when they create content and nothing happens, they question their strategy, change their tactics, pull out their hair, read more guides, spend money on training or mentors, and then, more often than not, after all that effort, stress and wasted money, they quit.

When you begin something new, you start from 0. It doesn't matter if your mum, sister, friends, partner or pet hamster are following you, their opinions are worthless. The only thing they can do to support you is to share all of your content on their social channels (as well as like and comment for social proof). If they really do believe in you (and like your stuff), they'll do that as a minimum.

The keyword for anybody in their first year of content creation is zero. The year is zero in your journey, you start at zero and you should expect zero results too.

Likes, comments and shares from your friends and family do not count. The only people who can lift you off zero are those you have never met, seen or spoken to.

Keep a track of the number of 'strangers' who follow your content. They're the only people who count.

Time is a human being's most valuable commodity, so when somebody (who you've never met) spends their most valuable commodity consuming your content, it's a privilege. You should feel honoured by every single stranger that makes your dial tick up from 0.

I want this to be every new creator's expectation from now on. Forget the views, shares and likes attached to the online guides, they've been won over years of effort. Your number is 0, it's what you've earnt, it's where you're at and it's what you deserve until you prove otherwise.

If you aren't able to adjust your expectations to 0, being a content creator is not the profession for you. Trust me, you'll go insane, become depressed, desperate and take a constant twinge of inadequacy wherever you go.

Until stated otherwise, you are zero.

Those people who expect too much will try anything to get their dial ticking. Many of them will question everything they're doing and constantly adjust their tactics. This might mean things like changing content type, content length, posting frequency and even their content quality level. By the time these people are done, they've tried everything in the book (they've even chucked the book at it) and all they've proven is how inconsistent they are.

And if there's one thing that will drag your expectation levels above the 0 mark (other than throwing cash at it) it's consistency...

18. I FEEL LIKE THE ONLY PERSON IN THE WORLD

It's 4.50am, my alarm beeps. I roll closer to my girlfriend, shut my eyes and prepare for the inevitable.

The alarm goes again at 4.55am. I roll away and begin a mental countdown from 5 to 0. When the count gets to 0, I swing my legs from the duvet and drag myself from the satisfaction of the mattress.

I head out of the room, empty my bladder, wash my hands and go down stairs.

It's 5.05am now, I won't be at the office for almost 4 hours, but this is my time. I feel like the only person in the world.

I flick the kettle on and wait, thinking about what needs to be done. My mind starts its first meaningful spins of the day.

The boiling water hits the ground coffee and the smell braces me for what's to come. I take it upstairs to the study, open the laptop and without a second thought, sink into something.

At the very latest, it's 5.15am now. My girlfriend will be

asleep for another hour and I'll stay at my desk for another 90 minutes at least.

I make the most of it, writing, thinking and strategising. There is no better time of the day for your brain to think creatively than first thing in the morning. The frontal-cortex (the part of your brain responsible for creativity) is more active immediately after sleeping, while the analytical parts of our brain become more active as the day goes on (and function badly this early). This stirs a perfect storm - a complete free flow of ideas, with no breaks for analysis, doubts or editorials (that could easily savage the purity of my ideas).

BTW: 90% of this book was written (or dreamt up) between the hours of 5-7am. What do you do between these hours every weekday? *(Check out and subscribe to my website for more 5am blogs: www.joshbarney.blog)*

The time is gone before I know it. It's 6.45am now. I'm satisfied with what I've achieved.

By the time I've brushed my teeth and got my things together it's 7am. I drive my girlfriend to the train station, kiss her goodbye and press on to the gym.

It's 7.15am when all my things are shut away in the gym locker and the key is wrapped around my water bottle.

After an hour's workout, I hit the showers, get dressed, say a passing goodbye to the old fella who disinfects the gym entrance and head out to the car park. A couple of the staff from our marketing agency are waiting by my car. Their eyes are bleary from sleep. I'm fresh, invigorated.

I drive the carpool into work, traffic depending, I'm usually in the office by 8.45am (9am at the latest).

I say my 'good mornings' (if anybody's in the office earlier than me), boil the kettle and drink my second coffee of the day, taking two minutes to get my head in the game, and then I begin.

^^^This is an average morning for me^^^

I'm not sharing this to show-off or to imply that I work hard (please don't patronise me with the 'hard worker' cliché), it's important that you see what a typical day looks like in my life, because you need to know what you're up against.

If you're a content creator, have just started with content (within the last 12 months) or are thinking about becoming a content creator, that's how I've got where I am. And I wish I'd found this consistency sooner.

When I started trying to maximise my days (because seriously, 24 hours are not enough) I felt like somebody was wringing me out like an old gym towel. Now that I'm through that stage, I would never go back.

Even as somebody who writes and conveys complex ideas and emotions every day, I struggle to explain what the mornings really mean to me, but for now, let's just call them my sanctum.

These small hours have given me an inner peace that I didn't know existed, but that wasn't the motivation behind discovering them. I wanted to get better, realise more of my potential and improve my life. Little did I know that I'd be training myself to become a machine.

Before most of you have woken up or even thought about completing any tasks, I have smashed out almost 2 hours of work that are better than anything I'm capable of achieving at my office desk. This additional time is how I'm able to write a book, grow traffic, build links, generate content ideas, strategise content, direct freelancers, outsourced and in-house staff, grow businesses online, distribute content, analyse and optimise businesses' performance across all channels, write and edit blogs, read and review submissions, read 100+ emails (and reply to approximately 10 of those) and a bunch of other stuff, every single day.

In other words, I've figured out how I can do as much work in 1 day, as most people can in 3. Yes, it means sacrifice, but it's been worth it for me (look at you, you're reading my book! Surely that's proof enough!).

It's much harder to build up speed than to maintain it.

It sounds conceited, but this is what I've had to do to get ahead in content marketing. If I didn't have this attitude, it would've taken 3 times longer to achieve the results that I have. And I don't have that kind of time. You might, but I definitely don't.

It's this kind of attitude, motivation to work and hunger to get ahead that will lift you off a deserved expectation level of 0. If you put in as much as this, I'll let you raise your expectations. You don't necessarily need to wake up as early as me (maybe you're a night worker instead) but you sure as shit need to work as consistently to prove yourself.

To many of you this might even sound monotonous or

slightly routine-y, but every day I do different things in the gym, different tasks at work, create different content, read different emails, adventure out into the unknown with new marketing tests. It's not a routine, it's a framework and I can't break from it. I need it. Every step is charged to give me momentum, to have me working at my maximum throughout the day, and besides, it's all structured to provide my content with the most important, magic ingredient...

...consistency.

Without consistency, you're fucked as a content creator.

Digital content is just like the content of any other medium, including television, radio, cinema, books, newspapers, magazines, etc.

And what do all the top performers in these areas have?

Consistency.

People, whether they'd admit it or not, like to know what they're going to get and when they're going to get it. They don't like surprises very much and they actually crave repetition (it acts as a safety blanket). And when you look back at some of the oldest content types (e.g. radio shows, magazines, television shows) it couldn't be more apparent.

For example, ask yourself:

- Does your favourite TV series ever vary in length? Do they suddenly change from an hour episode to 10 mins the next week? How would you feel if they did? Undersold?
- Do they erratically change the actors who play

the main roles in your favourite shows? If they did, what effect would this have on your connection with them?

- How often do they release an episode of your favourite TV show? Is it always at the same frequency whilst a series is being aired?
- Do they suddenly change the storyline of your favourite TV show? Do they skip from plot to plot without you knowing what's happened?
- Does the newspaper you read ever stop being published because somebody doesn't agree with a story in there? Do you think they have time to be hurt by people's opinions?
- Do radio shows stop being aired if they're new and their audience is small?
- Do the best movies consistently market themselves even after they've been released in cinemas?
- Do magazines stop being published because they've received an angry letter?
- Do your favourite magazines change their subject focus from week to week?

If you're serious about becoming a content creator, you simply must have consistency. It means that your audience know what, when, why and how to expect you. It means that when you finally manage to attract a few people's interest, they know where to find you, how often you'll be there and what you'll be doing. It means that they're able to share it with their friends and recommend you. It means that you can slowly, inch by inch, create something you can be proud of.

Consistency is NOT creating and publishing a ridiculously amazing long form piece of content, going quiet for 10 days and then posting something short with very little value.

Consistency is an unwavering commitment to quality, frequency and subject.

The three main components of consistency (in terms of content creation) are:

1. Quality
2. Subject
3. Frequency

When I refer to 'quality', I'm talking about the value that your audience can take-away after or during consuming your content.

This quality can come in the form of emotion, entertainment or education (to name a few broad quality types). It really doesn't matter what type of value you inject, how you do it or how much there is, what matters most is that you're consistent with it.

The more quality your content has, the bigger and better your audience will become, however, constantly chucking tons of quality into your content and being consistent with it will kill you. For instance, this book is filled with quality (it's probably the most valuable single piece of content I've ever created), but there's no way that I could create and publish a book like this frequently enough to sustain a decent presence online (at least not without any help from a team of content creators).

This is why you simply cannot create super-high value pieces of content all the time. You will burn-out quickly, run out of ideas and there will be massive breaks in your interactions with your audience.

The answer to this conundrum is a content creation sweet spot that ties quality and frequency. This sweet-spot gives you the platform to maintain a consistent presence.

The key to finding your sweet spot is to look at how much value is in your content. The lower the quality of your content, the more frequently you need to publish it, and the opposite goes for high-quality content.

For instance, if I was focussing on growing my Instagram and becoming an Insta content creator full-time, I'd have to publish new content at least once a day because an Instagram post doesn't hold much value. Videos on Insta are limited to just 60 seconds and images are limited to a maximum carousel size of 10.

However, if I wanted to become a full-time YouTube creator, I'd have a lot more options available to me. I could publish and create videos of 4-12 minute length 2-3x a week, 1x 60 minute video a week, or I could even publish 7x 2-3 minute videos a week.

Being a content creator is a constant journey, if you run out of content ideas or energy after 3 months, it's game over.

Remember, content with a higher value tends to take more time, so select your sweet spot carefully. Don't kill yourself by trying to produce super-high-quality content three times a day.

You must have a sustainable content plan that you can be consistent with, no matter what. If you're going for once a week, make sure you're there, if you want to do every day, don't drop the ball, if three times a week is your thing (my personal favourite atm) pick your publish days and stick with them. Just make sure you turn up when and where your audience expect you, without fail.

The other (and final) element of consistency is subject. To a seasoned creator, this point goes without saying, but to content rookies, it's their biggest kiss-of-death...

19. DO NOT BE THE PLATTE

The final element of consistency is subject.

Subject is something I need to cover in more depth, because a lot of content creators totally screw this element (without realising it).

In 1889, a time long before fake followers, hashtags and photo sets built like private jets, an American Journalist named Edgar Nye, shared his thoughts on an important waterway in the tributary system of the Missouri River. This notoriously shallow system was known as the Platte, and Rye used it to coin the now infamous phrase '*a mile wide and an inch deep*'.

This quote has been used in politics, academia and tons of other fields, because it is literally the epitome of career failure.

If you want to be a success, do not be the Platte.

The Platte is not exactly a great river (has anybody outside of Missouri ever heard of it?) and the term that Nye used to describe it, isn't a great compliment either. If you ever want to use this quote, here are a few appropriate applications for you:

- Somebody who claims to know about every-

thing, but actually has a very limited know-
ledge about all of it
- Somebody with no expertise
- Somebody who's abilities are entirely superfi-
cial
- Somebody who is very shallow

As you can see, being *'a mile wide and an inch deep'* sucks, but even if you are like the Platte, it doesn't mean you can't make it as a content creator, you just need to pretend that you aren't. Yes, that's right - more fakery.

This is the reason that subject is so important to consistency (and consistency is the bedrock of success).

If you're going to become a successful, money making and reputable content creator online, you must pick a subject and hammer it. Don't flick around, don't assume that people give a fuck about your real life and don't blur your content channel. Be consistent with your subject and it'll be crystal clear what your specialism is.

In other words, you need to:

Go an inch wide and a mile deep.

This kind of blinkered focus leads to mountains and mountains of bullshit content, but it's something that every content creator needs to go through to achieve their goals.

BTW: In terms of content creation, going an inch wide and a mile deep means relentlessly creating content about your niche, even if the information in that content becomes insanely specific at times.

When you focus as tightly as 'an inch wide and a mile

deep' you end up creating pretty shitty content that has very little meaning or purpose, but it works nonetheless (and aligns you closer with your chosen subject/industry/niche). It's like a hairdresser making a 10-minute video about how to style a basic quiff, or a vegan chef writing an entire blog about how to boil potatoes.

There is no getting around content like this. You need to keep creating content for your audience and you cannot abandon your subject when you do.

The gym and fitness corner of content creation is a clear exponent of this. I like keeping fit and I follow a few people that I consider 'experts' because I like their content, but occasionally they'll publish something that is the most mundane, pointless, waste of internet space I've ever seen. Stuff like how to move your arm when you're doing a certain exercise, how to keep your leg straight when you're doing another, I've even seen a video from a creator who was talking about why you shouldn't eat food while you're working out.

Content like this is complete and utter bullshit, especially when you see it from a creator's perspective, but equally, it's crucial to success.

A creator has to stick to all 3 points of consistency, no matter how niche their content occasionally becomes.

When content creators go into painfully specific (and pretty insignificant) detail, in the eyes of many audience members it actually positions the creator as more of an expert in their industry. It has a few other benefits as well:

1. Aligns the creator closer with their subject

2. Reminds the audience about their expertise
3. Allows them to keep up with the frequency and value of their content
4. Helps the creator remain relevant

These 'inch-wide, mile-deep' pieces of content fill gaps in all the top content creator's calendars because they're easy to make and have all the aforementioned benefits.

The creators who tend to fail online are those that are either too afraid or too naïve to spot the potential in content like this.

If you follow an up and coming creator from the start (which I try to do for my own analysis and research as often as possible) there tends to come a point between 3-12 months, when they either batten down the hatches and power through with all 3 points of consistency, or the wheels zig-zag, wobble on their axel and fall off. This period (almost always) begins with erratic content subjects and the topic of this change is usually centred around themselves.

When you create and publish content on a blog, YouTube channel or social media profile that focuses on something you're really fucking good at (e.g. health, aromatherapy, humour) you're going to have to prove yourself. If you let poor results get to you and you start shifting the focus of your content away from that thing, you're going to lose. This means keeping the limelight away from your personal life, until you've built an audience who really are interested in you.

People have their own problems, aims and entertainment values. When you're starting out, remember who you are.

Only create personal centred content
when you've earned the right to.

If you want to share something about yourself, do it on your own private social media channels (until your audience actually want it). Flicking between your focus subject, cat, fashion, family, dinner and favourite sports team, might make you think that you're being more personal, but it's wasted content space.

BTW: When a new visitor discovers your content channel 6 months after you began building it, you want it to appear as a highly focussed resource that centres around your subject. Not a confusing miss-match of topics.

Think about the topics that are most important to you, are there content creators or resources that you immediately associate with these niches?

For example, think of a creator, resource or brand that you instantly connect to any of the following subjects:

- Technology
- Sport (more specifically, your favourite sport)
- Celebrity gossip
- Travel
- Politics
- Positive thinking
- Marketing
- Gaming

This kind of topic-to-creator association is what you must try to achieve with your content channel (especially when you're starting out) and the only way you'll get it, is by being prolifically consistent with your subject.

When you know your niche, own it, keep hammering it, make it your own. Create bullshit 'inch-wide, mile-deep' content that's largely insignificant if you have to, just make sure you don't stop at it.

'The road to success and the road to failure are almost exactly the same.'

-COLIN R. DAVIS

20. THE BLUNT SPOON
OF CONSISTENCY

For most, their first year (sometimes their first two years) of being consistent comprises of nothing but failure.

Failure can consume weeks, months or years that you'll never get back.

Failing on a prolonged basis can do terrible things to a person. It can hurt so much that the things they thought they'd die for, mean nothing anymore. It can be so repetitively devastating that the values that they said they'd never break are smashed into a million tiny pieces.

When you're pushed into a corner and you're punched in the stomach over and over again, you're much more likely to duck out of the ring, than to keep taking punishment.

Every content creator must go through the process of failure. All of us have.

Unless your parents are celebrities (or very well off) you're going to have to fight hard and lose a lot. I've failed so many times that I've lost count. What do you want me to do about it? Cry? Give up? Moan about it in a book?

The best way to defeat failure is with more consistency.

The only way you'll get to the top is by being brave enough to keep putting yourself out there.

It shouldn't matter that you're getting 3 views, 1 like and 0 comments to start out with, everybody at the top has had to go through this. The top performers in every industry have failed (even after they've made it to the top)...

...Gordon Ramsey can burn a slice of toast, Roger Federer can be beaten in straight sets, Apple can release a terrible product and Beyonce can sing a note off-key, but we still regard these figures as the best in their space because they've beaten failure out with an unerring devotion to consistency.

When they fuck up, what do you think they do? When they perform badly, how do they react? When strangers criticise them with destructive comments and reviews, do they stop?

You must accept that your brilliant ideas will occasionally become terrible creations (and that this will crush your spirits), you need to know that people are bastards and some of them will intentionally try to dent your confidence, you must accept that even when you do something that is truly amazing, it probably won't get the attention or respect that it deserves (in your early years of content creation)...

...and that's because you're up against the Gordon Ramsey's, Roger Federer's, Apple's and Beyonce's of your industry.

The only way to beat them is to use their game against

them. It's to be the most consistent mother-fucker there ever was, to become a brick wall of emotion when your content fails and to beat through failure with the blunt spoon of consistency.

And when you do this, you, just like the people at the top of your niche, can put in an awful performance and your audience will still buy what you offer, forgive you for the mistake and turn up to see you again.

21. 100 DAYS FROM NOW I WILL BE A FEARLESS BADASS

It's time for another story of internet stardom, this one's about Jia Jiang (pronounced Jah Jahng, according to his website).

Jia's journey started many years before the internet was popularised. He was 14 and Bill Gates' was visiting his hometown of Beijing to deliver a speech. Jia found out more about his achievements and was inspired to become an entrepreneur and one day buy Bill Gates' Microsoft.

Spoiler Alert: Jia was never able to buy out Microsoft.

A few years later, Jia had the opportunity to move to the U.S and he took it, hoping that it would help develop his business (as it had for his idol, Gates).

Years past and Jia's business wasn't growing. In fact, by the time Jia was 30, he was a marketing manager at a Fortune 500 company but he still hadn't started up his own dream business.

Jia had worked himself up through the ranks, but he was unsatisfied because he'd procrastinated, cowered, was afraid of speaking out and was terrified that people would reject him and his business idea.

Jia isn't alone in this. Our lives are filled with people who say they want to achieve great things, but never get around to it. Fear has clogged 'digital graveyards' with content creators who weren't ever able to take the risk.

Fear will control you until you decide it can't.

Jia, like many of us, tried to look for different ways to overcome his fear. He studied books, searched Google and read blogs. The messages he found came in two different forms:

1. Psychological studies about what fear is and how to overcome it. These theories are amazing on paper, but much more difficult to put into practice.
2. Motivational content telling him that he just needed to start. Again, these messages are repeated heavily online and are much easier to say than do.

These things weren't enough for Jia. He kept searching and this is when he discovered a little-known online game. He fell in love with the idea and decided to take it further than anybody ever had.

Jia bought a website, prepped a camera (his mobile phone to begin with) and emotionally charged himself for the next 100 days.

He was ready to play his game and conquer his fears, one

day at a time. Every single experience in his game would be filmed as a 'vlog' on his mobile phone and written about in a short blog[19]. The entries are still all available on Jia's website.

BTW: This two-pronged content approach (written and video) is an awesome method of appealing to more people, generating a wider audience and increasing momentum (especially when you're starting out). Everyone has their preferences about content medium, some prefer to read, others like to listen and many like to watch. By creating the same content in many different mediums, a creator gives themselves a much better chance of appealing to more people.

Jia's first blog entry came on 15th November 2012, it opens with this paragraph:

'I am on a journey to become a great entrepreneur, drinking the smoothie blended with Steve Job's charisma, Chris Gardner's tenacity, Paul Graham's judgment, Bill Gate's ruthlessness, Warren Buffett's longevity, and Marc Zuckerberg's vision (or luck). However, since I'm not born with most of these traits, I need to acquire them through exercise, one-by-one.'

Although this might sound pretty out-there, it had nothing on Jia's next 100 days or the transformation that they would bring about in him.

Jia's game was called *'Rejection Therapy'* and the idea was to seek rejection at least once a day, for 100 days. The purpose of this strange sounding therapy is to desensitise the participant to rejection, fear and the pain of being turned-down.

Our biggest fears, especially when it comes to achieving

our aspirations, are rooted in what other's might think of us. The therapy works on the principle that if you were able to make these fears inactive, you'd be so accustomed to rejection that nothing could stop you. Or as Jia put it, '100 days from now I will be a fearless badass who couldn't care less about rejection or judgement.'

He began his first day of rejection therapy in a shopping centre. A very nervous Jia can be seen on the 1-minute video, nervously approaching a security guard, *"Excuse me..."* Jia says, *"...would it be OK if I borrow a $100 from you?"*

"No, why?" The security guard responded.

"No reason." Jia replied and scampered away.

And his game had begun. Although this short exchange might not sound like a lot, to somebody who is fearful of rejection, asking a complete stranger for $100 was the perfect way to begin.

From here, Jia faced all sorts of different challenges, some he dreamt up himself and many others suggested by his growing audience. Here are a few of my favourites:

- Going to a FedEx depot and asking them to send a package to Santa Claus
- Asking to do the weather forecast for a television company, whilst live on their news show
- Having a bike race (on a kid's bike) around a Toys 'R' Us store
- Buying a quarter of a shrimp (from a fishmongers)
- Trying to sleep in a mattress shop
- Sitting in the driver's seat of a Police Car

- Trying to interview Barack Obama (he was president at the time)

After 100 days and 100 challenges, Jia completed his very own version of rejection therapy in front of a very large audience.

Following his story, he spoke at a TED Talk, won awards, published a bestselling book, created a successful mobile app and is able to name brands such as Google, IBM, LinkedIn and Deloitte (to name just a few) as his clients.

As a content creator, it's crucial that you understand how important it is to accept failure, conquer your fears of judgement and develop total confidence in yourself.

In order to develop true consistency, you must not allow yourself to succumb to criticism or rejection, Jia's story is a great example of the success that anyone can achieve when they eliminate fear from their lives...

...and it leads us perfectly into the next chapter, which features something that all the greatest digital content creators must have in their armoury...

22. THE ENGLISH LANGUAGE HAS A LOT OF AWESOME WORDS

Have you ever seen those videos of snowboarders who fall endlessly down snow-lined cliffs before getting to their feet at the bottom like nothing happened?

How about those clips of surfers who are eaten alive by waves (that look otherworldly) only to float to the surface unscathed, 30 seconds later?

What about those boxers who get punched in the head repeatedly by some of the biggest, meanest bastards you've ever seen without even blinking?

Put yourself in their shoes for a moment. Do you think you could take that type of punishment and come out in one piece?

If not, do you think they were born with harder bones than you? That their bodies inherited genes that allowed them to be smashed on replay?

Or do you think it's something that their body has learnt to deal with? That they've become tougher because of the training they've had to go through? That they know how to get hit, or fall, or punched in the head, and take it on the chin?

The English language has a lot of awesome words, as well as some improvised ones that use prefixes to create opposite meanings (a prefix attaches to the front of a word to change its meaning), for example happy and unhappy, agree and disagree, legal and illegal. But sadly, there isn't one word that describes how these surfers', snowboarders' and boxers' bodies become stronger by putting themselves in harm's way, until the author, Nassim Nicholas Taleb coined it...

...Antifragility.

The word, as described in Taleb's book (Antifragile, 2012[20]), defines something that is the opposite of fragile. The book's opening paragraph sums it up perfectly:

'Some things benefit from shocks; they thrive and grow when exposed to volatility, randomness, disorder, and stressors and love adventure, risk and uncertainty.'

Being antifragile is not the same as being tough, resilient or robust. These terms describe something that can withstand painful exposure and remain the same. The antifragile actually becomes stronger when it is exposed to these same stressors.

Let's go back to the example of the snowboarder to explain why this is so important for you, and why I believe, that all of the digital world's top content creators are (or must become) antifragile.

As a snowboarder learns their trade, they fall down. It's

unavoidable. They don't want to, but as they develop their skills, try to go faster and practice new tricks, they inevitably fall. In their profession, it's part and parcel of pushing their boundaries and improving their skills. And every time they fall, they become better at it. In other words, the snowboarder's body is antifragile. It isn't tough or resilient, it becomes less fragile with every failure.

If snowboarders didn't expose themselves to the stress of falling, they'd never get better at snowboarding. Becoming antifragile is a by-product of improving their trade.

A content creator must understand that becoming antifragile is a necessary offshoot of publishing their work online, and that it's an incredibly powerful attribute that they should try to nourish.

The more content a creator publishes, the more antifragile they become.

I believe that we are all shaped in some way by our childhood. If, as a child, you were protected from groups of other children who might bully, tease, fight or annoy you, you'd be more fragile as a result. However, if you were exposed to this, you'd become the opposite in the face of these aggravating social circumstances.

And antifragility extends further than our psychology, it also strongly affects our physiology. When you were a child, was there a kid at your school who was wrapped up in cotton wool? Were they always excused from certain exercises because their parents were worried about them? Did they wear gloves and always bring in a lunchbox with food that was protected by 8 layers of cling film?

There was a kid like this at my school and he was sick all the time.

His parents' attempts to protect him, actually made him more susceptible to illness. In fact, even when he wasn't sick, he looked like he was on the verge of going that way again.

The fact that a vaccine is a tiny specimen of the very disease that we're trying to protect ourselves from, says it all. Who would've thought that the best way to become immune to smallpox, was to inject ourselves with a strand of the same virus.

Vaccines make our bodies antifragile, just as that kid (at my school) became more fragile as his parents tried to protect him.

BTW: Hiding yourself away from exposure (like the kid at my school) is known as naïve interventionism.

For the majority of creators, their biggest fear (or fragility) of creating and publishing content online, is what others might say about them.

Many of us never start the thing that we really want to do because it exposes us to results that are out of our hands, in the case of content creation, this is the opinion of others.

Your content might be laughed at, ridiculed, ripped apart, alternatively, it might be loved, adored and achieve amazing results. The fact is, you will never know until you are brave enough to expose yourself to the random event.

You need to learn to be that snowboarder who falls down every time he tries a new trick. Sure, you'll hit the ground, but every time you do, you'll become stronger because of it.

*You'll become more antifragile with every failure,
and unerringly consistent as a result.*

Don't aim to become sturdy or stubborn or even tough, become better with every negative bullet fired in your direction, be an antifragile content creator.

'To avoid criticism say nothing, do nothing, be nothing.'

-ELBERT HUBBARD

23. BEFORE WE GO IN ON INTERNET TROLLS

A quick message to anybody who has received negative feedback, is afraid of taking abuse online or is worried about what people will say about their work:

The more comments, views, engagement (in general) and mentions a piece of content receives, be it positive or negative, the more people the algorithms of the internet will show it to. This includes Instagram, Facebook, YouTube, Google, Twitter...

In other words, if you post something online and it does get tons of abuse, it's actually going to help you get more exposure.

All press is good press. Let the trolls come. The more they comment and abuse you, the more views you'll get and the more people you'll reach.

So, before we go in on internet trolls (which will be happening in the next section), just remember, when they think they're doing harm or trying to hurt content creators, they're actually making our content antifragile, let them do the same to you too.

24. A MENAGERIE OF DANCING TURDS

When I first started blogging, I fucked up with the whole troll thing.

The blog was about writing and centred around some valuable skills that I really wanted to share. I genuinely believed that my knowledge could help others and after some hesitation, decided to publish my first few articles.

Looking back now, they were pretty awful. In fact, given that I've only got better with experience, they were the worst things I've ever published online (and that's why I'm not going to tell you where to find them).

Your content is never going to be worse than the first piece you publish. It's the same for everyone.

When I started out, I didn't have an audience, the website was at complete zero, I had no social followers and no links or promo channels. I wasn't even brave enough to tell my friends! In other words, I started in the exact same place as everyone else.

My first plan was to get onto social media and share the blogs. To begin with, this plan centred around the world's most popular social network, Facebook.

BTW: Social networks are a pretty good place to start if you're trying to grow an audience.

As planned, I started sharing articles and nothing really happened. I gained a few likes here and there and generated a tiny inconsequential dribble of website visitors.

After about 5 or 6 posts, I received several notifications saying that somebody had commented on my latest post. I remember clicking on that notification thinking, 'This is it! Finally! I've got my first real follower! This is the start of everything!'

I couldn't have been more wrong.

The person (I can't remember his fake name) had left a series of GIFs on the Facebook post that shared my blog.

The first was a horse shitting out a mini mountain, right at the very forefront of the shot.

I scrolled to his next GIF, it was a short clip of Jeff Goldblum from the original *Jurassic Park* movie, removing his sunglasses and staring at a huge mound of shit left by a sick triceratops.

For some reason, I still hadn't figured out what was going on. I was too hopeful and my expectation levels were far too high (like all naïve content creators).

I swiped down to the final GIF, it was a man's cartoon head. His mouth was opening and tiny curled-up poops were running out of his mouth, with even smaller arms and legs waving in the air.

It was at this point that I scrolled back to the top and

squinted at it, 'Why would one person put these three GIFs on a Facebook post that promotes my blog?'

...10 seconds passed...

...and then it clicked.

Before I even knew what I was doing, I'd deleted his comments.

This was the first real feedback I'd had from somebody I didn't know and they were implying that my blogs were shit - not just once, three times! So much so, that they'd turned my Facebook post into a billboard of short movie animations, focussed solely on faeces.

A few minutes after I'd deleted his comments, the same guy published the same GIFs again. So, I did what all naïve beginners would do, I deleted the comments and blocked him from interacting with anything related to my page.

It was a bad move. Little did I know that I was actually playing into the troll's hands.

The person (I've been calling him a 'he' so far, but the troll could be either gender) didn't return on that post, but they did make me question whether I should continue publishing content online. I was already in a decent full-time job, fresh out of university and wasn't sure if I wanted to put up with abuse just for trying.

After a wobble, I decided to ignore it and get back to doing what I loved, creating content. Within a few days, I'd published my next blog and shared it on Facebook.

The blog could not have been on there for more than 30 seconds before the same GIFs appeared on the post, this time from somebody under a slightly different profile name.

I sighed, deleted the comments and blocked the new user.

They didn't return until my next post, when the same thing happened from another different profile.

This happened 4-5 times in a row. It got to a point where I was posting my blog and then waiting at my laptop to delete and block the troll. He was like clockwork (looking back now, he probably followed the page with a profile that he wasn't using for trolling) and he always taunted me with the same GIFs, in the same order.

It's at this point that every content creator has two options:

1. Let them win and quit what you're doing.
2. Realise what they are and just let them get on with it.

My attitude changed. Instead of feeling fearful or annoyed by his childish GIFs, I actually felt sorry for him. Every time he'd comment on my posts, he'd have to create a new profile, which meant registering a new email account and then making a new Facebook page.

This made me think about all the other people he must've been doing this to. How many had he beaten? How many had he successfully scared away from posting content online? And how many, just like me, had stopped giving a fuck about him? Because that's exactly what happened.

I stopped deleting his GIFs and just let them run on my

blog posts, I didn't even bother blocking him anymore.

On my next post, he added his usual 3 GIFs in record time. I saw them, grinned and just left them up there. A few hours later, he returned and posted another 10-15 GIFs. The comments section was chock-a-block with short, silent animations that were all focussed on shit (of course). It was a menagerie of dancing turds.

Still, I did nothing.

He came back again with more.

Again, I didn't react.

This determined and unrelenting trolling continued for another 5-6 posts. I didn't ever respond or delete them. I looked at them, saw them for what they were and laughed.

And then they stopped and I haven't seen those GIFs or that troll since.

(If you're reading this Mr Troll, thanks for buying my book! I hope you're enjoying it!)

The troll had quit coming after me because I'd taken his moment of satisfaction away. When I deleted his comments and blocked his new profile, he enjoyed it. It was like a cheap thrill, like he knew that he'd annoyed me and even though he'd have to go through the process of creating a new profile, the joy of pissing me off was worth it to him.

I must admit that I was sad when he stopped posting on my blogs though. Through his massive effort to get my attention, he'd actually helped my blogs get more exposure on Facebook. My posts were enormous moving faecal billboards, catching the eye of anybody who was scrolling through their Facebook newsfeed. By the time he'd given up, I was receiving about 5x the clicks (of my previous posts) and had generated loads more followers.

What the troll had used to destroy my posts, had actually made them stronger. He'd made my Facebook posts antifragile.

So once again, thank you Troll. I probably wouldn't be sitting where I am today if it wasn't for your help.

25. THE HEART
OF A PIGEON

I was fortunate with my early experience of trolls. Others have not been quite as lucky.

If you are planning on diving into the world of content, it's essential that I explain a little more about trolls, so you're armed and ready for them (if they show up).

Let's get this thing started by examining a very real fact about them:

Internet trolls don't get any sex, ever.

The closest thing an internet troll gets to sex is a 10-minute call with a semi-naked woman on any channel that starts with a 9.

It's essential that you know this about trolls. If you are ever targeted or suffer from the abuse of a hardcore troll, I urge you to return to this fact before taking any form of action.

Don't get angry with them, don't take them seriously, pity them.

Trolls are lonely little people, who sit in

dark rooms and touch themselves.

A troll doesn't want anybody to succeed in this world. They want a universe of complete failure. They want anybody who ever tries anything to suffer. They want businesses to go bankrupt. They want relationships to end. They want families to fracture. They want everything good to smash and break into pieces. They want all of these things, because they are deeply unhappy and they can't stand the idea of somebody else trying to achieve happiness. If everybody is hurting, they're on an equal level with the world.

Trolls will do anything to make others unhappy. This includes things such as:

- Performing thorough research on you
- Using information about your friends and family to hurt you
- Creating images or memes about you
- Repeatedly and relentlessly targeting you
- Ignoring pleas and desperate appeals for them to stop
- Using death, rape or torture threats to exert more influence

A hardcore troll really doesn't give a fuck about anyone other than themselves. Their sole aim is to hurt, harm and cause despair in others, without any thought of the other person's feelings or mental state. They feed off misery.

Just as a water balloon swells when you fill it with piss, a troll grows in strength and joy when it causes pain to others.

*If an internet troll does or says something
that hurts you, don't let them know it.*

The first rule of trolls is to hide pain, annoyance or frustration away from them. The biggest mistakes that cause trolls to thrive include deleting the troll's comment, retaliating with weak (or off the cuff) abuse or asking them to stop. These are all clear signs of pain, even if you try to mask it.

I was stupid enough to delete a troll's comments and had to put up with the same troll trying to suck me dry for months. Don't fall into the same trap.

Trolls have ended the career of many promising content creators, but immeasurably worse than this, is the number of lives they have prematurely ended.

To many of you, the idea of suicide motivated by internet trolling is far-fetched and almost incomprehensible. I felt the same, but after experiencing trolling (even in such a soft way) I can understand why those who are unprepared might succumb to such tragic actions (especially the vulnerable).

There are a few strategies that anybody can adopt in order to defend themselves and I'll get to those in a minute, but before that, I want to reveal a few more undeniable facts about internet trolls:

*There is nothing in this world uglier, more disfigured
and acne-ridden than an internet troll.*

If there's one thing that all trolls have in common, it's their disgusting appearance. Their faces are known to be so hideous that social networks, forums and comment threads do not allow them to use real photos of themselves. Instead of this, they use pictures of Kermit the Frog and V for Vendetta, or a photo of the opposite sex who they masturbate over several times a day.

Their hideous appearance allows them to remain anonymous online, which gives them more power, because:

*Internet Trolls have the heart of a pigeon
and the spine of a jellyfish.*

There is no creature who is more cowardly, fearful and yellow in real-life than a troll. They have itsy-bitsy metaphorical testicles, a non-existent character and although they're able to speak out on the internet, their tongue quivers so much in real-life, that they're unable to utter a word - especially when they have something negative to say.

This is one of the reasons that nobody has any respect for them in person, which is a shame because:

*The ego of an internet troll is so bloated, that despite
their tiny sexual organs, hideous appearance,
cowardice and complete lack of personality, they believe
themselves superior to anyone who ever existed.*

Internet trolls revel in the pain of others because they hate to see people surpassing them. How could anybody dare to improve their lives beyond that of a troll?

If you're trying to improve your life, you're probably going to get trolled. It's a sign that you're doing the right thing. Enjoy it, it's part of the process.

26. WHEN YOU REALISE YOUR MATES ARE IGNORING YOU LOOOOOOOOOL

In my experience, there are 3 different tactics that bring an end to trolling.

The first is to see a troll's comments, enjoy them for what they are and leave them exactly where they were posted. I am not telling you to ignore them, not at all, that would make you more resolute, I want you to use them to grow in strength. That means looking at them, watching them and measuring how they help you achieve your aims.

Remember the troll who targeted me? He helped me gain attention on social media, driving more clicks and followers, as well as giving my content the opportunity to impress new audiences.

Every time he posted a new, more shocking GIF, I felt the benefits. You can do the same. A troll's comments make good advertisements for your content. They are like bolt on billboards for your original content post.

The next way to destroy a troll is to kill them with kindness. I love this tactic. Sometimes it takes time to grind trolls down, but if you're really nice and quick to reply to their comments, you can completely destroy them.

It goes without saying that trolls are a force for bad. They're straight-up bastards, who add nothing positive to the world, so it makes perfect sense to slay them by being their polar opposite.

Deep dive into their profiles, look at their activity and see if there's any way that you can compliment them.

Every time I do this, I imagine the troll sitting in the darkness at their mother's house. They're waiting for a hurt reply, comment deletion or an angry response so they can feed on the power of upsetting others. But, just as they're prepped to feed, they get something like:
'Hey Dave, Just checked out your profile and saw that you're a United fan. My cousin loves them too. I hope they beat City at the weekend so you can celebrate. Thanks for the comment and have a good one! Oh yeah, and btw, awesome profile photo man!'

It's comments like this that make a content creator antifragile. It gives you an extra kick of confidence that's hard to find elsewhere. A troll will rarely reply to a comment like this, but if they do, go ahead and be kind again.

The third way to destroy a troll is to out-troll them. This is a good tactic for brands and businesses who receive derogatory comments from softcore trolls. However, I advise anyone who is targeted by extreme trolling to avoid this tactic, because a hardcore troll will only come back with worse and more extreme insults.

Trolls who attack businesses (instead of people, personal brands and celebrities) quite often show their real face and name. They're similar (in that they feed off other's misery) but they're less afraid of hiding because their victim is a collective, not an individual.

When you out-troll a troll in a public domain audiences take notice, and they love it. It gives a brand attitude, danger and a voice that's worth following.

Perform this tactic well and I promise that you'll gain followers and boost your performance on social.

You might be thinking, how am I supposed to out-troll a troll? Fortunately, there are a few businesses online that do a pretty exceptional job of squashing trolls, and I've gathered up a few examples of their work (on Twitter), for your viewing pleasure:

BTW: I don't want to give any trolls the pleasure of appearing in my book by name (they'll think they've won), so I'll just call them troll.

Troll (1):
When you call someone and it goes through to their Tesco Mobile Voicemail… LOOOOOOOOOOOOOOL

Tesco Mobile[21]:
@Troll When you realise your mates are ignoring you LOOOOOOOOOOL #nojoke

Troll (2):
Immediate turn off if a girl's mobile network is tesco mobile

Tesco Mobile:

@Troll Are you really in a position to be turning girls away?

Troll (3):
Worst thing about me mother not answering her phone, is her voicemail reminding me that she's on the absolute poverty Tesco Mobile

Tesco Mobile:
@troll Nah the worst thing is your mother blatantly ignoring your calls

Troll (4):
@Wendy's you're food is trash

Wendy's [22]**:**
@troll No, your opinion is though

Troll (5):
Why do y'all eat at @wendy's? their nuggets and burgers ain't shit smh

Wendy's:
@troll delete your account

BTW: The Wendy's Twitter profile is infamous online, with people regularly contacting them just so they can be trolled in return. They've used the trolling of their account to build a massive troll themselves and their audience love it. It's tongue-in-cheek, funny and different to other businesses.

Troll:
@Wendy's Roast me

Wendy's:

@Troll Get one of your 51 followers to roast you.

27. WHERE THE PERSON BEGAN AND THE SHIT ENDED

When you consider the amount of bullshit that a content creator has to face online from their peers and their audience, it's easy to see why we quickly become full of shit.

So far, you've discovered the mounds of bullshit content a creator needs to separate themselves from, the lies and fakery of other creators, the rejection and ignorance of their audience and the pain and hurt of merciless negative feedback.

If anybody had that much shit chucked at them in their working day (which for beginner creators is usually in their spare time at home) they'd be covered in so much shit, that nobody would know where the person began and the shit ended.

And as the opening few paragraphs of this book tell you, even those creators who make it to the top are mentally battered, beaten and bruised by a combination of these shit throwing factors.

If the opening of this section hadn't given it away already, it's time we entered a dark and twisted place - a content creator's mind.

Content creators are the (shit) artists of our time.

I know that I've criticised and ridiculed content creators who use fake tactics, copy others and generally live a lie, but here's where I offer an understanding hand.

Let's go somewhere that few others have been brave enough to dare...

28. A PUBLIC BADGE
OF DISHONOUR

A creator's success is measured in numbers. This is done by tracking comments, likes, shares, followers, traffic scores, leads, sales and engagement (amongst other things).

This isn't anything special. In fact, almost any job can be quantified (put into numbers) and compared with historic, peer or competitor performance to measure success. For instance:

- A sports person's success can be measured in wins and goals.
- A salesman's success can be calculated in actual sales
- An accountant's success can be determined by the size of the accounts they manage (and therefore, the amount they can charge for it)
- A fireman's performance can be evaluated by their response time and the percentage of lives they have saved
- A teacher's ability can be measured in their classes' exam pass rate (and average grades)

Numbers make sense for us to track because they're easy to understand, compare and analyse. They don't require lengthy explanations and they make decisions bite-sized for time-short managers.

However, in the world of content creation, the numbers that track our performance can have severe mental repercussions. The reasons for this are twofold:

1. They're public

2. They're a popularity contest

When you combine these factors, you see why a content creator's numbers can have such harsh and biting effects on their character and mentality.

For starters, everything a creator does is with the aim of attracting and impressing other people. These popularity numbers can be particularly damaging, especially for people who are unaware of the world they're entering.

Imagine how a creator feels when nobody likes their stuff, not just once, but 100 times in a row. Do you think this has an effect on their mood, confidence and personality?

A creator's unpopularity and social rejection isn't tucked away either. They wear these numbers like a public badge of dishonour and the only way they can hide it is to delete their content and start again.

The very public nature of their content's disapproval (and the complete ignorance of their audience) can lead to some pretty awful things in a creator's mind.

And what worries me even more, are the number of

young people who not only aspire to become content creators, but the growing percentage who are actively attempting to break into the profession (especially as 'influencers').

BTW: I'm not saying that young people shouldn't try to become content creators. They just need to know what to expect before they put themselves out there.

The percentage of teenagers on social media has never been higher and coincidentally, mental health problems and suicide rates in this demographic are at an all-time high too.

A recent report (2017) from the Office of National Statistics has revealed that suicide rates in children and young people (aged 15-19) has increased by 67% in 7 years (since 2010)[23]. These numbers are insanely high and although we cannot pin them all directly on social media and digital content, it's clear to see a correlation between the two.

Stats like these aren't isolated to the UK either (where I'm based) this pattern has spread wherever social media (and content marketing) has reached the youth of today.

We have created a world that is reliant on likes, shares and followers for social acceptance, and these numbers are publicly revealed to everyone.

For those of us who are ill-equipped to deal with rejection, it can lead to irreparable mental damage and explains why so many content creators (particularly those in the formative stages of their careers) suffer from mental health problems.

Another study in 2017 was undertaken by the Royal Society of Public Health[24] (RSPH) about the impact of social media on the young people of today. The study asked 1,479 young people (aged 14-24) to score a variety of social networks - positively or negatively - on a host of different factors. These issues included:

- Anxiety
- Community building
- Body Image
- Depression
- Loneliness
- Self-identity
- FOMO (fear of missing out)
- Sleep
- Emotional support

Five of the world's most popular social networks were selected, with the participants scoring each network for every factor in the study.

BTW: This study refers to young people as 'digital natives'. A term used to describe people who have never known a world without the internet.

Of all 5 networks, only 1 of them came back with a positive score, the remaining 4 were judged to do more harm than good. And the one network that was thought to have a positive impact on young people's lives, only just scraped above a 'net negative' result.

The results were as follows, with the most positive at the top (and the most negative at the bottom):

1. YouTube

2. Twitter
3. Facebook
4. Snapchat
5. Instagram

YouTube was the only network that resulted in a 'net positive' result from the study, with it scoring particularly well for factors such as 'Health Awareness', 'Self Expression' and 'Self Identity'.

Interestingly, YouTube is the only network on the list that is formatted in a very different way to the others. It has no newsfeed, doesn't feature heavy levels of content from personal connections and YouTube's content cannot be consumed in a matter of moments (their videos are longer!).

At the very bottom of the pile is Instagram, which came a long way back in terms of negativity (even from 4th placed Snapchat). Insta scored incredibly low scores for 'Body Image', 'FoMo', 'Anxiety' and 'Depression', but scored the best (of all the networks) for 'Self-expression'.

Instagram has quickly become the most popular network for young people and aspiring content creators. And whilst sites like YouTube are vastly popular in the youth of today, only a small percentage of people who use the video network produce their own content. Insta is quite the reverse of this, with almost all Instagrammers posting their own content.

On the face of it, it's easy to see why a social network like Instagram could inflict so much damage on young minds. Users are constantly bombarded with beautiful images of perfect, successful, highly attractive joyful people, and the creators who share images like this aren't all celebrities or flourishing Insta content creators (although, these people really aren't helping matters), many of them are their own friends and families, who, as is the competitive nature of the Instagram culture, have tried to replicate and outdo others with their content.

Throughout our lives, we are psychologically programmed to seek approval from others. As children, we seek the approval of our parents, but as we grow into teenagers our need for approval shifts onto our peers and friends. This is an insanely stressful and awkward psychological period of our lives that now includes the 'perfect life' content of Instagram.

Young people who use the platform face a difficult choice, conform to social pressures by creating content that seeks approval (and show-off) or seclude themselves altogether from this type of content and outcast themselves at a very sensitive stage in their lives.

Every year we hold a world mental health day and social media explodes with supportive messages from content creators, and although many of these creators suffer from problems themselves (and openly talk about it) the very next day they return to publishing a beautiful photo of themselves beside an infinity pool, under a crystal blue sky.

These content creators know the damage they're causing, but they can't break from it. They're trapped in a whirlpool that keeps dragging them back in.

I have spoken to a few content creators (and Insta influencers) during the creation of this book, who are ethically and morally-minded. They say that they want to escape the pressures and fakeness of their posts (and I believe them) but despite this, no matter what they do, they can't stop posting perfect-life content.

The reasons are clear. The bullshit sinks further than skin deep. It's in the chemicals that travel through our veins...

29. A BIG OL' CLUSTER FUCK

I know I've made a few controversial statements so far, particularly to anybody who is involved in content creation, but I think that this one will top them all:

I want less people to like, comment, share and consume my content. And I want the same to happen to you too.

Like I said, probably the most controversial thing I've said so far...

On the surface, this sounds like a pretty emo comment. It's basically an admission that I want to perform worse at my job, but of course, that's not the case. Every day I aim to perform better than the last and fulfil my potential, and I work extremely hard to achieve that goal.

The problem is that the ultimate purpose of a (proper) content creator lives in massive conflict with the steps they must take to get there (and measure their success). It's a bit like trying to reach the summit of a mountain, whilst having to hike downhill the entire way.

What many creators forget is that they only exist and succeed in their jobs because their audience support them.

My ultimate purpose is not to make money or become famous, it's to serve my audience. I want to educate, entertain and excite the people who back me with their time and money and this means making their lives better.

If your main aim as a content creator isn't to improve your audience's life, quit now.

This doesn't explain my desire to reach fewer people with my content, nor does it clarify what I really mean by that statement. The truth and real reason for this, lies in the type of visitors and followers that digital content attracts.

A content creator's like, comment, share and follower numbers are not entirely genuine. A lot of these 'users' (who perform these social actions) are only engaging because they've been programmed to do so. They aren't liking my stuff because they really, truly, deeply enjoy it. They're doing it because they're addicted to it.

The reason for this isn't ego-driven (although this definitely contributes), it isn't worsened by boredom and it isn't caused by Instagram influencers who fake 99% of their lives, it lies in a chemical that's released every time we log onto social media, receive a mobile notification and post content about our own lives:

Dopamine.

Dopamine is commonly thought of as a 'happy chemical'[25]- a substance that is released in our brain to make us feel good. Whilst this is kind of correct, the function of dopamine is actually a lot more complex.

BTW: Dopamine's purpose as a neurotransmitting chemical was first identified in 1958 by Arvid Carlsson and Nils-Arp Hillarp at the National Heart Institute of Sweden[26].

When you do something you enjoy, dopamine is released to inform your brain that you're experiencing pleasure. The more dopamine, the more happiness you feel.

But, dopamine isn't finished there. It's also released when you think about something that you have enjoyed before and are anticipating experiencing again (or long for). In some cases, more dopamine is released in anticipation of an event than when that event actually takes place. For example, think about the last time you booked a holiday, was the excitement of booking the holiday matched by the holiday itself?

BTW: Typical activities that release dopamine include eating good food, sex, monetary rewards and winning awards/competitions.

It's for this reason that dopamine is able to condition our behaviour[27]. We do something we like - dopamine is released, we think about doing it again - dopamine is released (driving us back to the original stimulus).

In all forms of addictive drugs and behaviour, a huge amount of dopamine is released[28] and when a drug or behaviour is able to tick these 3 factors in terms of dopamine release, addiction is almost a nailed-on guarantee:

    1. *Speed*: The quicker the release of dopamine,

the more addictive the stimulus. This is why substances that are smoked or injected capture a more intense dependence than drugs that are swallowed.

2. *Intensity*: The more dopamine that's released in one hit, the greater the chance of addiction.
3. *Reliability*: The more reliable the source as a stimulus of dopamine, the more addictive it becomes.

In layman's terms, when we enjoy something, our brain releases chemicals (dopamine) that beg us to do it again and the better, quicker and more reliable that experience is, the more our brain begs.

Have you ever known a self-confessed addict (maybe you are one yourself) who has proclaimed time and time again that they were going to kick an unhealthy habit but failed repeatedly in their attempts?

Dopamine affects (to name a few):

- Smokers
- Alcoholics
- Gamblers
- Drug addicts
- Junk food addicts
- Gamers (computer game addicts)

Adictive habits like these can be harmful to our welfare, but something else happens to our dopamine release as we keep up with our addictions...

The more we experience a stimulus that releases dopamine, the more the brain limits the amount of dopamine that's released when you experience it. Basically, the more you do something, the less pleasurable it feels.

This is why smokers remember their first cigarette, drug addicts associate their first 'hit' as their best and gamblers hunt for the feeling that their first big win gave them. Unfortunately, these 'highs' are almost impossible to achieve, so we smoke more, drink more, take larger quantities of drugs and gamble larger sums of money in search of the feeling that dopamine drives.

But dopamine isn't done there. As we become reliant on an addictive stimulus, more dopamine is released in anticipation of experiencing it again. So, even though the experience is less pleasurable, the chemical tells us to want it more.

In other words, it's a big ol' cluster fuck.

The power of the chemical is real, present and serious. In the 1950's a pair of scientists, Olds and Milner[29] (who sound like a comedy double act) implanted electrodes in the brains of rats.

The electrodes were hooked up to levers that gave the rats a tiny dose of electrical stimulation to certain areas of their brain. The animals were given free access to these levers, and after experiencing the effects of the electrical stimulation, did not have to press any of them again.

The rats could've avoided the levers altogether, and therefore, not shocked their brains again...

BTW: Don't try this at home.

...but the scientists discovered that the rats actually wanted to press levers that stimulated certain areas of their brain. One of their participants enjoyed a lever so much that it shocked its own brain 7500 times in just 12 hours.

Can you guess what was released when the rats shocked this part of their brain?

Yep, you guess it, dopamine.

We might not be rats, but the chemical has been proven to have the same reward-based conditioning effect on us.

As you might've guessed, a ton of different studies have revealed that dopamine is released every time you log on to social media, post content about your life and receive notification from them[30].

Social networks are reliable, fast-acting and hard-hitting sources of dopamine for new users, but as time passes, the experience becomes less about being social and more about the relentless chase for dopamine.

I know that a lot of the people who like my stuff on social media do not even take the time to read it. Many of them do not even know what they're doing on social media or how they got there. You'll see these people everywhere you go: blankly staring at their mobile phone, tirelessly running their fingertip up the screen, scrolling through social media posts with no real purpose. They'll tell you that they're doing this because they're bored, but it's really because dopamine has turned them into social media zombies and they're unable to enjoy a moment's peace.

I don't want that for my audience. Yes, I want you to follow me, share my stuff, read and enjoy it, but more than anything I want what's best for you and if that means less social numbers on my content, so be it.

It's important (to me) that I earn your likes and follows, not be handed them by dopamine addiction, but as you're just about to find out, I'm one of a very small group of people who think like that...

30. SOMETHING IN COMMON WITH JUNKIES

Before we get any deeper into this dopamine thing, I need to remind you that I don't dislike social media, the internet or content creators.

Social media is a gift for the world.

Social media and the internet in general is a force for good. Every day I learn new things, am amazed by eye-popping content and entertained by some of the internet's most incredible creators. Twenty years ago, none of this would've been possible.

Before the internet, the content we consumed was controlled and directed by the few. Content was available to us via television, radio, magazines and newspapers, which were controlled by a small group of people.

These small elitist groups would decide what content we'd consume and who'd be able to share it. Our choice was limited and controlled by these decision-makers. If a particular writer wasn't in favour with the editor, he'd never be published, if a comedian was deemed unfunny by a television channel, we'd never know about them, if a natural educator didn't have the channel to share their wisdom, the world wouldn't be given their lessons.

The internet and social media in particular, has allowed people who would never have made it on our historical content channels, to flourish and share their greatest qualities with the world. That's a gift, despite all the bullshit we've covered so far.

The internet is the world's great leveller.

I love the internet and the opportunities it has given us, however, just like all amazing tools, we need to know how to use it for good.

When content creators first grip the starter cord on their career and ready themselves to rip that engine into gear, very few are prepared for the tool they're about to wield.

Full-time content creation is like a game when you start out. All you want to do is share content that stays true to yourself and yet, you end up on a relentless chase for likes (and followers/subscribers). Every time someone looks, likes, shares and comments with positive messages, it feels like a shot in the arm.

These engagements aren't harmless, they release dopamine and over time, this conditions our behaviour.

Content creators are addicted to internet engagement.

I am not afraid to say that I'm heavily addicted to social media engagement, internet traffic figures, lead capture numbers and most worryingly, the highly addictive power of dopamine.

In a normal working day (in the office), I will have the

live analytics figures of the websites that I'm working on, open on one of my desk's screens (either laptop, mobile or desktop computer), does that sound healthy to you? The analytics don't change because I'm watching them and yet, when those stats spike it gives me a tiny buzz that I cannot get enough of.

To anybody reading this who isn't a pro content creator, it's similar to posting something on a social network, or sending a message in a group chat, and then checking your phone every 30 seconds to see who has liked or replied to it. No matter how many times you check, it won't affect the number of responses, and yet, certain messages cause you to do it over and over again.

If you do regularly check back to count the likes on your social posts (or see how many people have looked at your story) imagine how it feels when you post a piece of content to an audience of 10k, 100k, or 1 million. If you thought it was cool sharing a post with 500 followers, try multiplying that 20x and experiencing the dopamine effects, and then try doing this numerous times every single day (of your working life) on a variety of different channels. Do you think this might fuck you up, even just a little bit?

There are a ton of negatives to this kind of addiction (which I'll cover in a minute), but there are some positives too.

For starters, it feels fucking awesome. Imagine creating something based purely on your ideas, posting it online and then seeing 1,000's of people sharing it on social, even more liking it, 10,000+ viewing it on your website and to top it all off, you receive tons of ego-stroking emails and messages from strangers. Sounds cool, right?

A content creator has something in common with junkies. They'll never forget how good those first few likes felt.

A content creator who has grinded their way up to this level deserves to enjoy it. This is how all the hard hours, frustrations and under loved content is repaid. However (speaking from experience) the enjoyment is only temporary. The dopamine effects lessen with every piece of content you publish, until you're almost completely numb to it.

Publishing content just becomes a process that still drives the same compulsive actions (the constant checking of your stats and engagement) but with barely any enjoyment.

I was in this position about 12 months ago and no matter which way I turned, I just couldn't explain what was happening. My content was performing better than ever and our audiences and engagement rates were sky-high, but I felt empty to it all.

It was weird because this is what a content creator dreams of when they start out - a huge, growing audience, who love their stuff and just want more of it. I'd worked insanely hard to achieve these aspirations and yet, I felt empty when I'd (pretty much) achieved them.

Dopamine had worn me into a shell of what I was, not in terms of performance (I knew more and was better than I'd ever been) but in terms of job satisfaction, life quality and mental state.

It was about a month later (and 4 weeks of research

and reading), that I figured out what was going on. When I understood what was happening, how the addictive (and then emotionally numbing) effects worked and the reason I was performing in such a robotic way, I was able to take control of it.

When you understand the cause of addiction and know why it's happening, it becomes controllable. Whenever I feel underwhelmed or indifferent to my content's performance, I look back to old data.

BTW: Analytics programs save data for years, meaning that I can literally step back in time and look at my website's performance from 3 years ago or view seriously old posts on social media to check out engagement stats.

A quick look and comparison (with what my content is achieving today) is a great reminder of how far I've come and my reasons to be grateful.

If you're a creator who is dazed, deadened or insensitive to the amazing numbers that you're achieving, check out your old stats and try to remember how you felt when you were starting out.

'I have absolutely no pleasure in the stimulants in which I sometimes so madly indulge. It has not been in the pursuit of pleasure that I have periled life and reputation and reason. It has been the desperate attempt to escape from torturing memories, from a sense of insupportable loneliness and a dread of some strange impending doom.'

-EDGAR ALLAN POE

31. THE DRUG DEALERS OF THE DIGITAL WORLD

Addiction fucks people up.

It's thought that as many as half of all acquisitive crimes (e.g. burglary, fraud, shoplifting) are the cause of drug addiction. That's an astronomical £2-2.5 billion a year in stolen goods in the UK[31] (market value, not street value).

Think about the number of deaths and serious injuries alcohol causes every year (especially with regards to driving), consider the pain, consumption of our healthcare system and number of early deaths associated with tobacco, think about the emotional pain and mental state of a gambling addict who has begged, borrowed and stolen money from others to fund their addiction.

These are major (and quite terrifying) examples of the selfish nature brought on by addiction and whilst they might be far removed from what we're about to look at, they are still aligned with the same common behavioural traits.

Just as an addict might ask to borrow £20 for food and then take it to the local off-license for a bottle of vodka, a creator can lie just as shrewdly.

As already explained (a lot earlier) content creators can bullshit about their follower numbers, post likes, settings, life, experience, knowledge, creativity, almost anything, to get what they want. And although a lot of these tactics sound awful, cringy and incredibly devious, many of them are actually the result of addiction. This doesn't make their actions better, but to a certain extent, it makes them a little more understandable.

The longer you're in the game, the less exciting it gets. This means less dopamine, less happiness and less hunger. Every time you post a piece of content, the engagement buzz weakens. It's like those first few likes are worth 10,000 of the ones you generate further into your careers. This is dangerous and it's the reason why so many businesses sell deception (e.g. fake likes) and have made a killing this way.

When a creator's buzz has been squashed, they need to work so much harder to get it back. They need to get more likes, comments, shares and followers than they ever have before. Their content isn't giving them the quick fix of gratification (and the dopamine high) that it used to, so they have to amp up their efforts to achieve it. This is like an alcoholic who used to get happily drunk on 6 pints, but now has to sink 20 in an effort to attain that same joy.

For some creators (the honest ones), this means posting more content. The creators that chase this tactic believe that they can multiply their social (and content) gains by multiplying their content output. For example, if a creator is publishing one new piece of content a day, and it's getting them 500 likes and bringing in 5 new followers, then by doubling their output to 2 posts per day, they should get 1000 likes and 10 new followers, right?

Unfortunately, content doesn't work like that.

Time is our most valuable commodity and people always act in a way that prooves this. If you try to take up too much of your follower's time (by posting tons of content) they'll ignore you, unfollow you or worse still, tell others that you're a 'spammy' creator.

For example, is there anybody amongst your 'friends' or 'connections' on social media who posts (or shares) loads of crap? Have you thought about unfriending them? I have. I've unfriended a lot of people like that.

These people are amateur content creators who are addicted to social media engagement in the same way as the pros. They post (and share) tons and tons of shit (quite literally).

A professional content creator who keeps upping their posting frequency has the same problem. They want more likes and followers, without considering the human beings sitting on the other end of the screen.

BTW: When someone is spamming you, it feels satisfying to remove them from your life. Don't be that person.

In most cases of creators upping their posting frequency (beyond their audience's ability to consume it) it only ends one way - a straight loss.

A content creator who increases his social output without considering his audience is addiction driven.

I'm not deploring those who run tests on frequency, I've

tried every posting schedule in the book (as a test on my audience), but those who bullishly assume that their audience should spend twice as much of their precious time interacting with their content every single day, are in it for themselves, not the people who will make them.

As annoying as these people are, at least they're honest. Yes, they're trying to wring their audience out for every last drop of attention, but they aren't trying to deceive, as many others do.

Over the course of a creator's career, they might be forced to stir up a little hyperbole here and there, it comes with the territory (everyone else is doing it). However, the problem isn't in the single post, we can all excuse a one-off mistake, it's what the post causes that's the problem.

If I meet up with some friends that I haven't seen for a few years and tell them that I drive a Ferrari, I have to continue that lie every time I see them and the lie snowballs.

The same goes for a content creator. People aren't stupid, if they notice that a creator is lying to them, they will publicly lynch them online. This has happened to tons of creators, who have naively assumed that 'nobody will notice', only to take a backlash from their followers and the digital community.

BTW: If a creator lies online and gets caught out, they become a huge target for trolls and memes.

I'm sure that having to live a lie absolutely sucks, but this is still not the biggest problem that a content creator faces. When they take their first steps into the world of 'fake' and lies, a creator (if successful) will give themselves a boost in engagement. In simpler terms, their bullshit pays off. This is great for them, they get the buzz back and content is exciting again. However, it corners their options for future content.

Creators who use deceptive tactics become trapped by them.

When content lies pay off, a creator pays a heavy price. If they want to achieve the same results again, instead of working up to them (like everyone else), they'll have to cheat again...and again...and again...and again...and... you get the picture.

A lying creator's addiction for social engagement often spirals out of control and causes them to not only rely on, but also become addicted to fake tactics. This is why so many 'businesses' have sprung up in the last few years, offering every type of social and digital fakery, and worryingly, they're making serious money from it.

The creators who use them are not only destroying an industry and harming the success of their fellow creators, they're also feeding a booming corner of profiteers, who are happy to leech off the desperation of these (social) addicts. These people are the drug dealers of the content world and they're ready and waiting in broad daylight.

If you are in content (or you're thinking about it), know what the dopamine buzz is and never forget where you started. There are a million and one honest ways to hugely increase your following and social engagement - lying, cheating or faking doesn't have to be one of them, because when you start, it's almost impossible to stop.

32. I'VE BEEN PLAYING IT FOR 8 HOURS STRAIGHT AND I SWEAR MY EYES ARE BLEEDING

Imagine being the creator and owner of a piece of content that becomes the number one of its type in all genres (and categories) in 53 countries. Imagine publications like *The Huffington Post*, *The Telegraph* and *Mashable* reporting about its meteoric and unexpected rise to fame. Imagine this one piece of content earning you $50k a day without you even having to get out of bed in the morning.

This is exactly what happened to one content creator, but why did he remove it from the internet less than 28 days after the world went bonkers for it? Why cut-short all that earning power? That popularity? That fame?

To find out, let's rewind to the beginning of this journey.

In 2005, a young developer based in Vietnam by the name of Dong Nguyen, set-up his own video game development company called dotGears. For the first 7-8 years of its existence, there isn't a lot to tell. The company released a few games with little fan-fair or success. It wasn't until 2013, that the real story started for Nguyen.

In April 2013, Dong revealed on his Twitter that after just two days of creating a mobile game[32], it would shortly be available in the Apple App Store. The game was called 'Flap Flap', and the tweet that announced its arrival said nothing more than *'New Simple Game. Flap Flap'.*

After a month of silence and still no release, Dong posted a tweet that read, *'OMG! I scored 44 pts in #flap-flap!!!'*

Dong had made a mistake that he'd correct in his next tweet 2 minutes later. There was already an app named 'Flap Flap', so Nguyen had to rename his game to something else, the tweet that announced its arrival was *'Flappy Bird is out now!'*

And that was it, the now legendary Flappy Bird game came into existence on 24th May 2013.

In its first 5 months, Flappy bird only attracted 13 reviews and very low download figures, but something happened at the end of October that tipped the balance for Flappy Bird - it ranked in the Family Game category of the App store in 1459th place.

BTW: This might not sound like a lot, but to a marketer it means visibility. Think about the type of person who would scroll that low in an app store's game ranking list: die-hard mobile game addicts. These are people who will leave reviews, tell others and post content on social. This is a potential snowball moment for the right game.

Momentum picked up and Flappy Bird began to spread. The first ever tweet to mention its name (not from Nguyen's account) was posted on November 4[th][33], it read:

'Fuck Flappy Bird'

This was a message that millions would share just a few months later.

The tweet was not only apt to the difficulty of the Flappy Bird game but also demonstrated why it would become such a hit. Nguyen had created a game that was enjoyably frustrating and impossible to complete. This delicate (and hard to achieve) mix compelled people to take to social to share their experience.

Fast forward 10 days and the Flappy Bird avalanche was starting to roll. Nguyen's game had risen to 393rd in the Family Games category (moving up by more than 1,000 places) and entered the Game charts (for all genres) reaching 1368th overall.

Over the course of the next month, Flappy Bird more than doubled its review count and continued to gain traction on social media. By mid-December, Nguyen's creation had risen to the top 15 of Family Games, the top 80 of all games and even the top 250 of free apps in the U.S.

Flappy Bird Madness had begun. Here are a few Tweets that demonstrate this short stint in time:

User (1):
@dongatory So you're the creator of Flappy Bird? Thank you. Thank you very much. Because of you, I have no life.

User (2):
It's official...flappy bird addict. I hate it so much and can't quit playin it. #flappybirdmeltdown

User (3):
Flappy Bird is going to be the death of me #flapflap

Tweets like this were a huge social media trend at the time. Anybody who had the game felt compelled to tell others how annoying and difficult it was.

By early January 2014, Flappy Bird was number 2 in Family Games, number 6 in All Games (for U.S.) and the 8th most downloaded Free App in the iOS App Store. But still, the momentum did not slow. Flappy Bird's downloads were increasing at an astonishing 136% day-on-day, and on 17th January, Flappy Bird become the number one most downloaded free App in the U.S. (above the likes of Facebook, YouTube, Google and Instagram).

The game, that had only taken 2 days to create, had achieved something that nobody would've expected, and to top this all off, it was before Nguyen had even released a version to the Google Play Store. On 22nd January he did exactly that, releasing Flappy Bird to Android users, and within a week, it was the number 1 most-downloaded app on these devices too.

Nguyen's game held number 1 position for both Apple and Android users (in the US)[34]. An amazing feat for an indie game creator, who had taken on huge companies with teams of 10,000+ and beaten them.

But still, the meteoric rise of Flappy Bird wasn't over. By the 25th January, more than 500,000 tweets per day mentioned the game's name[35], and at the start of the next month, Nguyen's little Flap Flap game was the most downloaded game in 53 countries (iOS), bringing in $50k from ad impressions every day.

To a creator of any type of content, this sounds like a dream - a viral piece of content that keeps growing, doesn't require any attention or work, holds the number 1 spot (in its category) in 50+ countries and all the while, is earning serious money.

However, things were spiralling out of control for Nguyen, and within a week, he'd have removed Flappy Bird from the App store indefinitely.

Nguyen had reached the top and as a creator, he wasn't prepared for what happened next (he should've read this book first).

Other indie game developers started trolling him, saying that he'd bought reviews, created Flappy Bird fan pages himself and plagiarised Nintendo's artwork. The media picked up on these comments and published articles focussing on the same suggestions, The Telegraph and Newsweek published features that questioned Nguyen's success. Kotaku (one of the world's most popular video game blogs) published an article with the headline: *'Flappy Bird is Making $50,000 A Day Off Ripped Art'*[36].

Nguyen replied on Twitter:

It is hard to believe, I understand. I have no resources to do anything else beside uploading the game.

On top of this, the frustrated, angry tweets continued to pour in from the public. What had started as fun and tongue in cheek, had begun to take their toll on Nguyen. This Twitter reply pretty much sums up Dong's outlook:

User:
FLAPPY BIRD HAS RUINED MY LIFE! I'VE BEEN PLAYING IT FOR 8 HOURS STRAIGHT AND I SWEAR MY EYES ARE BLEEDING

Dong Nguyen:
It's just a game. Take care of yourself first. I don't make game to ruin people's lives.

The game's inventor admitted that he was receiving death threats and repeated harassment from people who claimed to both hate and be addicted to Flappy Bird. Nguyen took to Twitter again:

I can call 'Flappy Bird' a success of mine. But it also ruins my simple life. So now I hate it.

And a few hours later, Nguyen released this message to his followers:

I am sorry 'Flappy Bird' users, 22 hours from now, I will take 'Flappy Bird' down. I cannot take this anymore.

It is not anything related to legal issues. I just cannot keep it anymore.

And true to his word, on 9th February, Flappy Bird was removed from all App stores. After 50 million+ downloads, and 16 million+ tweets, Nguyen had had enough.

BTW: When Flappy Bird was removed from app stores, people sold mobile phones with the game pre-installed for stupid amounts of money. One phone listed online fetched bids of up to $90,000 [37]. Flappy Bird truly had sent the world mad.

Later, in an interview with *Forbes*, Dong would reveal that it was the addictive nature of the app that caused him to discontinue it, "Flappy Bird was designed to play in a few minutes when you are relaxed. But it happened to become an addictive product. I think it has become a problem. To solve that problem, it's best to take down Flappy Bird. It's gone forever."

Having been in a position where he could have earned $15 million a year (based on $50k earnings per day), Nguyen ended the Flappy Bird craze as quickly as it had begun.

Nguyen's decision to end Flappy Bird was a brave one that caused much more abuse, furore and anger. And as we know now, despite his best efforts, it did little to stem the world's addiction to mobile phones and social media.

33. A CASE COVERED IN LIGHTNING BOLTS

Before we leave the whole subject of addiction and the bullshit ramifications it's had on content (and the digital world as a whole) I want to chuck in a few hundred words about a subject that fascinates me.

Ever heard of the word, nomophobia?

If you haven't, can you guess what it means? The clue's in the name.

BTW: This is a legitimate word that I am not responsible for inventing. It doesn't even come up as a spelling mistake in my word processor document.

You might've guessed that it represents a fear, but have you figured out exactly what that is?

Nomophobia is a term used to describe a fear of not having a (functioning) mobile phone with you, and it's a very real problem for the young generation of today (no-mobile-phobia).

Have you ever lost your mobile phone? Broken it? Left the house without it? Or even put it in a separate room to charge?

When one of these things happened, how did you feel?

If you've ever had a weird panicky, anxious feeling of being lost or alone when you haven't got your mobile phone with you, you have experienced nomophobia.

Most people who have to deal with nomophobia, feel so uncomfortable that they do everything in their power to get that phone back again. This makes the simple process of charging it in a separate room a mammoth task, causing most people to constantly check up on it.

I remember when I got my first mobile phone. I was a teenager and mobiles were just gaining popularity. It was a Nokia 3210. Remember them? I thought I was the bee's knees when I had that thing (especially when I put it in a case covered in lightning bolts). This mobile, that would be considered a clumpy brick in today's world, had only three functions that were any use to me:

1. Text (from girls and friends)
2. Calls (from my mum telling me to come home when I was out too late)
3. Snake (smashing records when I had a few minutes to kill)

These were the days when we wouldn't get our mobile's out in meetings, or over dinner, or during a conversation, we wouldn't stare at them for hours on end, we wouldn't walk around the house with them in our pockets. We didn't constantly revisit them when they were charging. These were the days when we'd even turn them off in the cinema.

We used these tools to their maximum without allowing them to affect the quality of our life and mental welfare.

I'm not saying that I dislike modern smart phones. I think they're amazing devices, but do we overuse them? Yes. And does that have a serious effect on our health? Absolutely.

BTW: A report states that the average smartphone user has 3 hours and 15 minutes of screen time on their mobile phone every day (2018)[38]. That's more than 20% of our waking lives, staring down at our mobile phones.

If you're one of those people who:

- Get a sense of panic when your phone is misplaced
- Sleep with your phone within arm's reach
- Believe that your phone has rung or vibrated when it hasn't
- Puts your mobile phone on the table when you're in a meeting, having dinner or talking to someone
- Feels anxious when you're low on battery or out of signal
- Uses your phone whilst driving

...take it easy. Turn your phone off at night and put it somewhere that you can't see for an hour a day. Trust me, you'll feel like that same phone provides you with so much more value when you separate yourself from it (just a tiny bit).

I know this means that you'll consume less content, but it'll make the content you do consume (e.g. the videos you watch or blogs you read) so much better. You'll only see the stuff that is most relevant to you and it'll make the experience much more enjoyable, not just more 'meh'.

And before we leave it at that, I've got another new word for you to guess at, 'phubbing'.

Any ideas?

Similarly to nomophobia, this is a combination of words that have been pushed together.

Phone + snubbing = phubbing

This happens when you ignore someone (or don't hear them) because you're too focussed on your phone.

We've all been guilty of phubbing at some point, but serial phubbers are known to have extremely short attention spans.

If your phubbing gets out of hand, stop it (unless you're reading my content). Remember, you're a real person in the real world first.

34. THE WORLD'S MOST VALUABLE FREE RESOURCE

Content is the world's most valuable free resource.

The amount that people 'expect' for free from brands, businesses and individuals has moved so far from where it was, that the marketing world of twenty years ago is almost unrecognisable.

Think about the world of content 20-30 years ago. If you wanted to learn something new, you'd have to go to the library or buy a book, if you wanted to watch something, you'd have to wait for it to come on TV, buy a video or go to the cinema, if you wanted to read something by a particular writer, you'd have to buy the magazine or newspaper that they contributed to, if you wanted to listen to a certain piece of music, you'd have to wait for it to come on the radio or buy the cassette (or CD).

Now think about the world today. How do you access all of these content types? If you want to learn something, you use Google for free. If you want to watch something, you use a streaming service or go on YouTube for free. If you want to read something by a particular writer, you visit their blog for free. If you want to listen to a certain piece of music, you go on YouTube for FREE (or find a music streaming service).

*You must give away a lot for free to make
any money as a content creator.*

Notice anything in common with all the content types of today's world? They're all free (obviously), but also, they're instantly available. We don't need to wait for anything anymore. If we want something, we can have it.

BTW: We're going to come back to the subject of instant gratification (next), because it's too big and important a subject to skip, but for now, let's stick with the idea and ramifications of free content.

If you need an example of how far the free line has moved, look at the fitness and workout industry. I was a kid in the 90s, and at that time there was a device that every household had to have - a VHS player. This awesome piece of tech boasted a play and pause button, a fast forward and rewind function and a record operation (that would let you copy stuff from the TV).

BTW: If you left a VHS at the end of the tape after watching it, you'd have to rewind all the way back to the beginning before watching it again. This could take 30 mins on a crap VHS player. Good times.

Alongside the VHS player, there was a particular type of VHS that literally every household had – the fitness workout video. These aerobic workouts were big bucks back in the 90s and every Christmas, a host of (desperate looking) celebrities would release a workout routine. Included in these celebrities are names like Jane Fonda, Cindy Crawford, LaToya Jackson, a 76-year-old Zsa Zsa

Gabor (and her now infamous routine 'It's So Simple Darling', check this video out on my website www.joshbarney.blog), Cher, Mark Wahlberg, Carmen Electra (I wish I had this when I was a 13-year-old) and Fabio (it goes without saying).

When this was the only option available, people were more than happy to part with their hard-earned cash in exchange for 30-60 minutes of mundane exercises.

Let's compare that with today...

Do you know of any celebrities who have their own workout routines? I can't think of many, there are a few reasons for this:

1. Experts on fitness now have a voice
2. Celebrities aren't authentic authorities on the subject (most people will believe that they're copying the routine from their personal trainer, who is the real source of the valuable information)
3. It's hard work to make decent money from fitness content. Either you're all in or not at all.

Creators who compete in the fitness niche have an extremely hard task on their hands because there are so many people in that space who are happily giving away tons of stuff for free. This includes entire workout routines, specific exercise training, diet plans, workout schedules...you name it, you can have it for free thanks to the internet.

Content that has previously made people millionaires, is now expected for free.

The success of a content creator depends heavily on their ability to give stuff away without asking for anything in return (except maybe a follow or to 'subscribe'). And the more valuable the stuff that a creator is able to hand out, the bigger their audience will become.

35. I OWN THE FREE LEMONADE IDEA

If I stood on the street and gave away lemonade for free every single day, over time I'd build a big ol' audience of people who kept coming back to me for the same free treat.

BTW: In this analogy think of the 'free lemonade' as content, and the 'street' as your digital location (social profile, website, etc.).

If you saw me doing that and wanted to build your own crowd of people, you'd probably try to copy me.

However, doing the same isn't good enough in the world of content anymore, because by the time you start (my free stuff has made me):

- A trusted source of lemonade that people like— my followers already know the quality of my free content and they want more of it.
- A queue of other people, proving that my lemonade is bad-ass (social proof). As a creator it is much easier to acquire new audience members if you've already got a massive audience (100 new followers to a creator with 50k

is easy, 100 new followers to an account with 1,000 is much more difficult).

- Loads of other 'creators' who have already copied my free lemonade idea (and are failing at it)

In this example, I own the free lemonade idea. If you stood on a street and gave out lemonade, people (who had already seen or heard of me) would think of me.

*Own your content ideas or out-compete
others with their own.*

If I do start giving away lemonade, this is where my niche's line for free stuff exists. In order for you to be competitive and actually grow your audience, at the very minimum, you must give away something that is at least of the same value as my lemonade.

BTW: The free line is a creator's way of measuring their niche's minimum content value, so they know how much value they must put into their own free content for it be successful.

*Measure your content value against those of
your niche leaders and then surpass them.*

Your best hope (in the lemonade metaphor) is to either:

1. Steal my idea and own an interpretation of it, e.g. instead of giving out lemonade for free, you give out chocolate bars of the same (or higher) value.
2. Copy my idea and out do it, e.g. give out two lemonades for free, instead of one.

These are the two ways that you're able to compete

with other creators (in terms of giving away value for free).

The content world is constantly upping the levels of free, and the 'free line' is forever moving further into the realm of paid products and information.

As a creator you must understand and analyse the value that others are giving away in their content. Creators can measure this by looking at things like video length, educational lesson value, blog quality, production qualities, settings, featured products, the calibre of a podcast (or music), amongst a ton of other stuff.

A great example of this are eBooks. Several years ago you were able to charge a decent amount of money for these online, but now the free line has consumed a lot of them. (Unless you're selling them on Amazon, and this still requires loads of different factors to align for an eBook to be successful).

I currently have 6 eBooks that I give away for free online. They're all gated (this means you have to become a subscriber to get them) but nonetheless, I don't charge a single penny for them. Each one has:

- 25-100 pages
- Images and designs
- Step-by-step guides to achieving very specific goals
- Tons of valuable insights- some of the most valuable tactics and strategies that I've learnt online (aka stuff that you'd normally have to pay for)
- Resources

- A professionally designed Front cover
- A contents page
- Branded design on every single page

An eBook like this typically takes between 0-2 weeks to write, in addition to the cost of a designer who brings it all together in an attractive package (which normally takes a week to turnaround). By the time they're complete, I'm out of pocket in time and money, and I don't ever recoup anything directly from these eBooks. But this is where the free line is in my space, and if I want to compete, it's what I have to do.

This doesn't just apply to my area of content marketing; the same rule goes for every type of content creator in every niche. For example, a YouTube audience expects videos to have high-quality standards, and if it doesn't, they won't watch it (it isn't giving them enough for free). Would you watch a YouTube video in 2020 that has bad sound? Or has poor video quality? Or hasn't been edited properly? Do you think these things come for free?

And most importantly of all, what about the time creators put into planning, creating and editing their content. Should that be valued at zero too?

All of these factors highlight a clear movement in the content 'free line'. When YouTube was still a burgeoning platform, creators might have been able to get away with poorly shot, lit and recorded videos, but not anymore - expectations have changed. And those expectations cost creators (like me) money.

Being a content creator is like being a business, you have to invest money to make money further down the line.

If you're thinking about taking the plunge into serious content creation, I'd advise you to take a long-hard look at your industry, analyse the costs involved and take baby steps.

If you want to become a travel blogger, figure out if you can afford to live, travel and buy all the necessary recording, editing and publishing equipment first. If you can't, you need to adjust your target niche accordingly - for example, how to travel Europe on a shoestring budget (whilst being a travel influencer).

The fact that most influencers in luxurious niches (like travel and holidays) have come from privileged backgrounds, says everything you need to know. Do you think the average 22-year-old is taking their partner on holiday to 5-star resorts in the Maldives with recording and camera equipment that costs $5000+?

If you don't have the money, you need to be clever with your focus, angle, medium and content delivery to surpass the free-line in your space.

36. ULTRACOMPETITIVE GAME OF CHICKEN

Creators are constantly pushing the free line back to boost their audience size, trust, loyalty and engagement, and every time they do, it's fucking annoying for everyone else in their industry.

As a content creator, I'm up against a ton of adverse factors, but when somebody comes along and outdoes my one (metaphorical) lemonade with two, I have to react and increase my content value to match. This happens all the time.

If you'd like to see how this works, visit your favourite creator's page and scroll through their historic content. Go back months or years and measure the value of their content back then to where it is today. In most cases, you'll see new 'show' types, expansions into other formats (e.g. podcasts), the occasional longer form content piece and a general higher level of quality (more educational or entertaining than before).

To outsiders, this looks like a content creator getting better at their game, but to somebody involved in the industry, it's a clear indication that a creator has been forced to up their level.

At points in my content career, I've seen other creators go 'one up' on my stuff and felt like I'm in an ultra-competitive game of chicken. It's like we're pushing each other to go further onto the main road, dodging the cars of bankruptcy and risk.

All these increases in content value lead to major competition and sadly, the biggest winner is usually the one who can afford to invest the most in their content. This is true of almost any industry, but if you're prepared to stick it out and play the long-game (with consistency) of giving away free, valuable stuff, you'll make it to monetisation...

37. DIRECT ACCESS TO A GROUP WHO TALK ABOUT LEMONADE

I'm sure it sounds dumb to give away free stuff for months (and years), but it's the only tactic that will work for a content creator.

Creating value packed content and giving it away guarantees a few very specific things:

- To tire you out
- To wear down your resources
- To be copied and outdone by your competitors
- To grow an engaged, loyal audience

Yes, there are tons of negatives to constantly donating your knowledge and expertise to the world, and it's back-breakingly hard work sometimes, but it's the bottom bullet-point on that list that makes it all worth it.

Giving away free stuff develops an awesome audience who want to hear from you.

When you consistently give away valuable stuff, you

(gradually) build an audience who keep coming back for more.

There are some blogs that I visit at least twice a week, there are YouTube channels that I check on (almost) every visit to the network, there are podcasts that I always listen to at the gym or in the car, there are social profiles who's posts I always check out - and I'm sure that this is the same for you.

These creators don't just have you as a follower or channel visitor, they have your attention, and attention is something that can be monetised.

All the free content that a creator gives away is paid back when they earn the attention of enough people.

To understand how this works, look at your content channel like a machine. Every time you publish a piece of valuable content, you effectively put £1 in that machine, and over a year, that machine constantly eats your money without giving anything back. But one day, after a long time of you feeding it coins, you go back to that machine and there's a £50 note sticking out of it.

Every single time you publish a valuable piece of content, you make an investment in your earning potential.

The long-term value of giving away free stuff is immeasurable. When you get it right and begin to earn back the time and money you've invested in your channel, it's like no other feeling. Only a successful content creator can describe what it's like to earn money from something that they've been doing for free (out of enjoyment) for so long.

There are a handful of different ways for you to monetise an audience's attention. You will have seen them all online at some point. To help me explain how they work, let's go back to my free lemonade example.

If you remember correctly, I'm standing on the corner of the same street everyday (this is my website or social channel) and I'm giving away lemonade (my valuable content) to a crowd of regulars (my audience/followers).

I've been doing this for a long time now and the crowd have become massive. The same people return every day to see me, and many of them are even there before me, waiting for me to turn up with my lemonade. I realise that it's finally time to make some money out of this.

I have several options here, let's run through a few, what they mean and their pros and cons.

Put a Price on My Lemonade

This is the most obvious tactic and also the biggest mistake I could make. Instead of giving away my lemonade for free, one day, I try to charge the entire crowd for their cup.

A small percentage of my crowd will be happy to pay for my product, especially if I've proven its worth, but the vast majority won't.

By the time I've built an audience who I'm able to monetise, my free lemonade tactic is being used all over the place. Other creators have seen how I've built a big crowd and they've done the exact same thing. If I try to charge my audience for it, I'll lose them to my competitors forever.

The perceived value of my lemonade is also very low in my crowd's mind. I have been giving it to them for free for so long, that they associate its value as £0.

Content creators who try to charge their audience for the same content that they used to build that audience, fail 99 times out of 100.

Pros of pricing your previously free stuff:

- The audience already know how good your content is
- The audience trust you

Cons of pricing your previously free stuff:

- Content doesn't stay unique for long. Other creators will rip you off and offer the same stuff for free (whilst you're trying to charge for it)
- The content has low perceived value because it's been available for free for so long
- Low profit margins and unit price – if you try to charge a high price for a previously free product, you'll sell nothing
- You lose the majority of the one asset that you're able to monetise- your audience's attention
- You give your competitors an opportunity to steal your audience away for good

Allow Brands to Sponsor My Lemonade

Instead of charging the people who turn up to drink my free lemonade, I charge a business to sponsor my lemonade.

This might annoy a few of my die-hard regulars who don't want to see me 'selling out', but my lemonade is still free for the people who have become my most valuable asset - my audience.

There are a number of ways for me to use sponsorship to monetise my lemonade, I could place the sponsor's logo on the side of all my lemonade cups, rename my lemonade to include their brand, wear a t-shirt with their brand name or put a big banner up behind my stall.

It would be easy for me to sponsor everything and monetise as much as possible, but I know that this will annoy a lot of my audience. Instead, I must find a level of sponsorship that earns money and maintains my audience's trust and respect. This is also in the sponsor's best interest, as higher audience engagement means more brand attention, and a potential long-term partnership with my lemonade stand.

Sponsorship is an amazing way for content creators to monetise. However, it requires a large audience (which takes a long time) and a personality that a brand will be happy to align themselves with.

Pros of content sponsorship:

- High earning potential
- Zero monetary impact on audience
- Capacity for long-term financial partnership

Cons of content sponsorship:

- Can be perceived as 'selling out'
- Potential for brand sponsor to impact and direct content value and type

- Poor sponsor choice can ruin authenticity, trust and respect from audience

Ask for Donations for My Lemonade

I put up a sign on my stand, asking for my audience to donate to my lemonade stand. Included on the sign, I write a heartfelt message that says the lemonade costs money and any donations to help me cover it will keep the lemonade coming for years.

This tactic will have very little impact on my audience's size or attention levels, but equally, it will bring in very little money.

My diehard-regulars, who absolutely love my lemonade and have been drinking its sweet goodness for years, will donate in a heartbeat. How much they're able to give depends on their background, but it won't be a lot and it also won't be very regular. They might make a one-off donation, but they'll drink a lot more of my lemonade before they donate again.

The donation makes these diehard-ers feel a lot closer to my lemonade and to me as a creator, which is great. I have more of their attention, and they'll tell a wider audience about me.

However, as great as this is, I probably won't be able to make a living from these donations. If I had a huge crowd, I'd do alright, but even with the very big crowd that I have, I don't really have much chance. It's better than nothing, but that's about it.

If I was aiming for a different type of monetisation tactic, but my audience wasn't quite ready for it yet (e.g. a sponsor), donations could be the thing for me. This tactic won't affect my audience and it will bring in a small amount of revenue while I'm still growing.

Pros of asking for donations:

- Very little impact on audience attention
- No obligation for audience members
- Will make donators feel closer to me as a creator

Cons of asking for donations:

- Low earning potential
- Irregular and inconsistent source of monetisation
- Not sustainable
- Seen as desperate if done in the wrong way

Sell My Influence on Lemonade Drinkers

The crowd that I've built up absolutely loves lemonade, so I can be pretty sure that they all adore sweet treats and soft drinks too. This is valuable information, particularly to a business who sells products in this area.

If I was to monetise by selling my influence, I would recommend (or be seen using) a product that was relevant to my current crowd of lemonade drinkers. This could be as simple as me recommending it every time I hand out a glass of lemonade or visibly holding it in my hand (and using it). Whatever I do, I must make sure that I use the respect and attention of my audience to highlight how awesome this product is (and influence their decision to get one).

This can work really well if my audience feel close to

me, as it'll feel like a recommendation from a friend.

The closer I am with my audience and the bigger they are as a group, the more a company will be willing to pay for my influence over them.

If I was really clever about this, I'd learn as much about my lemonade drinkers as possible. I'd want to find out their ages, their genders, their average incomes, their jobs, their interests, hobbies...the more I learn about them, the more valuable my audience becomes. This is because I can prove to other businesses that I can influence my audience in their niche too. For example, it would be easy for me to be an influencer for a cherry-ade company (because we know my crowd all love soft drinks), however, if I found out that they all also love a particular type of shoe, a brand in that area would be willing to spend their marketing budget on my lemon-ade stand too.

The more businesses that I am able to attract, the more money I can charge every time I give away lemonade. Higher demand means a higher price for my influence.

Selling my influence could be a very profitable way of monetising my audience, however, I must ensure that the product recommendations do not overshadow my lemonade. The lemonade must remain my number 1 focus if I am to maintain my audience's attention. After all, it's the primary reason that they all show up to my stand every day.

Pros of selling your influence:

- Profitable method of monetisation
- Consistent and reliable form of income when

done correctly
- Free stuff!
- Can appeal to a wide range of businesses (if you're clever about it)

Cons of selling your influence:

- Can be seen as a sell-out
- Potential to ruin or overshadow your main content value

Sell Branded Lemonade Stand Products

My crowd are digging on my lemonade and it feels like I've built a real community.

Instead of charging for lemonade, I offer lemonade stand t-shirts, hats, badges, cups and hoodies. All of these products feature my lemonade logo and the same catchphrase that I say every time I give out lemonade: 'Have a sweet one!' The merchandise sits behind my lemonade stand and every now and again, I remind my audience that it's for sale.

Selling my lemonade stand products doesn't affect my audience's attention at all. In fact, some of them even think I'm a little bit cooler now, especially because I took some serious time over the designs and quality of my merch.

Sales begin well. The diehard fans immediately buy a few of my products and it makes them feel even closer to my brand. However, the rest of my audience are unsure. Sales are a bit hit and miss, occasionally I do very well and sometimes I sell none at all. I'm finding it tough to monetise like this consistently and I can't rely on my diehard fans to repeatedly buy my merchandise.

On the plus side, people are actually wearing my merchandise in public! This means that more people are seeing my logo and slogan, and hopefully, this will bring in more audience members and interest around my lemonade.

Merchandise is a very popular tactic amongst content creators, especially those with relevant slogans and quotes, but it's inconsistent, making it an extremely tough way for small creators to monetise.

Pros of merchandising:

- Elevates your brand's 'cool' factor
- Physical promotion of your content
- Very little negative effect on the attention of your audience (if any)

Cons of merchandising:

- Can come across as egotistical if done incorrectly
- Inconsistent earning potential

Selling Advertising Space Around My Lemonade Stand

An easy way for me to monetise my lemonade is to sell advertising space around my stand. I could sell one large advertising space, lots of little ones, or a combination.

Advertising will generate income, but I will need a lot of people to see it in order for me to become financially dependent on it.

I will also need to be careful that the adverts don't annoy or ruin my crowd's experience. If the ads are irritating, in-your-face or splashed absolutely everywhere, it's likely that it will put a lot of my audience off. But as long as I don't overdo it, I'm sure they will understand.

I put advertising up around my stand and try my best to avoid ruining my audience's experience.

I quickly discover that my adverts earn money for each visitor that sees them and as my audience size is pretty consistent, I'm able to earn a reliable income from advertising. But, as nice as it is to have a regular income, it isn't enough for me to make a living.

Selling ads is different to sponsorship, as a sponsor acts in collaboration with my business. An advertiser doesn't care about my lemonade, they just want to get their message seen by as many people as possible.

Pros of selling advertising space:

- Reliable form of income when the audience are consistent
- Minimally affects my audience's experience (when done correctly)
- Variety of places that I can sell as ad space

Cons of selling advertising space:

- Low earner unless your audience are massive
- Can ruin the audience experience when overdone
- Advertisers have no interest in your content, their aims are 100% their own
- Can be seen as a sell-out (if ads are too noticeable)

Make My Lemonade an Affiliate for Other Businesses

I don't need to earn money at my lemonade stand to generate an income. I could become an affiliate for other businesses, earning a percentage of every sale that's directed from my lemonade stand.

I set this up by getting a code from another business, and whilst my crowd are at my stand, I recommend their product and hand out the code. Anybody who visits the business will get a small discount if they use my voucher. And every time somebody buys from the affiliate business (with my coupon), I earn a small cut of the profit.

This tactic doesn't have a massive impact on my audience, however, I have to make sure that I don't push the affiliate product too much. The best way to do this is to recommend it to my audience (not sell it). The crowd already feel close to me and are prepared to give me their attention, so I make the most of it by telling them that the product is awesome.

It's important that I actually believe in the affiliate product and have tested it myself. If I direct my audience to a product that turns out to be a rip-off, is poorly made, or run by a company who don't care about customer service, I'll lose their trust forever.

However, if a content creator is able to find a high-quality product that would improve the lives of their audience, it's a win all around. A creator doesn't need to worry about orders, deliveries or admin after a sale is made. All they do is take a cut of the profit.

Pros of becoming an affiliate:

- Potential for highly-profitable partnership

with another company
- Little effect on audience experience (when done correctly)
- Could become a creator's sole income channel

Cons of becoming an affiliate:

- Your reputation is at risk if the affiliate product or company is sub-standard
- Smart members of your audience will notice what these affiliates are and might tell others, or question your trustworthiness (if you aren't upfront about it)
- The right affiliate products can be difficult to find

Make a Funnel From My Lemonade Stand

This method is an amazing way to maximise the value of all my audience members.

A funnel works by creating a monetisation route that increases in value with every step for the buyers. Some people won't ever take a step into my funnel and will keep enjoying my free lemonade, others will buy the first tier, some will get all the way up to the third. The key to a funnel is that the steps cannot be skipped, e.g. the 2nd step is only available to people who have bought my 1st step.

A funnel for my lemonade stand might look something like this:

1. Free lemonade (already available to everyone)- £0
2. Premium lemonade with special lemons- £1

3. Case of premium lemonade with special lemons- £5
4. Queue jumper privileges, get my lemonade before everyone else and have direct access to a special group who talk about lemonade- £10
5. Premium membership to my lemonade stand. First to drink lemonade every time it is released, case of premium lemonade every month and complimentary cup- £25 subscription per month (12 month minimum)

By creating this funnel, I'm able to maximise customer value as much as possible. For example, if one of my customers has only £1 to spend, they're still able to buy something (step 1 and 2). Likewise, if somebody has £500 to spend, I am also able to maximise their spending power (steps 1, 2, 3, 4, and 5).

This type of monetisation method works well for my lemonade stand, but after a while some of my audience seem to think that I'm only out to earn their money and decide to boycott my stand. These people go directly to my competitors and I don't see them again.

Pros of building a funnel:

- Maximises customer value
- Allows for upsells and downsells
- Can become a creator's sole income source

Cons of building a funnel:

- Can look like a scam to your audience (when done badly)
- Must create many products or services to monetise (and layer them)

- Can take the focus away from the quality of your free content

38. YOU'RE A SELF CENTRED, GREEDY, UNCARING, EGOTISTICAL, MISERLY BASTARD

When it comes to monetising a content creator's channel there is, as you'd expect, a whole heap of bullshit involved.

For starters, the average content creator cannot look like they're out to earn any serious money from their content (even if they are). In most cases, I'd advise that honesty is the best policy, but when it comes to money, tread very carefully.

It's OK for a creator to tell their audience that they need to raise funds for more content, or for their living expenses, or to cover their bills (without being desperate or letting it overshadow the content) but if you openly say that you want to earn expendable income from the content you're creating, you're dead in the water almost every time.

I know that you've been handing out free stuff (entertainment or education) for ages, I know that you've spent tons of time and energy building your content, I know that you've been super consistent and you've never let your audience down, I know that the equipment has cost you a small fortune and I know that you've had to put up with abuse…

…but if you tell your audience that you've done it all to make dough, they'll think you're a self-centred, greedy, uncaring, egotistical, miserly bastard.

And that's the truth.

Everyone in your audience knows that at some point you're going to use your content to make money, but none of them want to hear about it.

It takes a long time to build an audience but just one wrong move to destroy it.

Being a content creator can be a bit like being on a snakes and ladders board. When you're making content for free (before monetisation), there are ladders on almost every square you stand on. You keep on skipping up in size, having to work hard but seeing results snowball (after finding your consistency), but when you turn the corner with a big audience and want to monetise, it's like every other square has a snake on it, ready to drag you down.

This very precarious situation requires a high-level of bullshit that master creators are dab-hands at.

The secret to it (and my biggest tip) is to just ignore it's even happening. Don't acknowledge anything unless you're paid to. Yes, you can say things like, 'buy a t-shirt to keep my channel going' but don't ram it down your audience's throats. As long as you stay quiet about the monetisation method, most people won't say anything.

Keep your bullshit levels high when
you're ready to monetise.

You'll also find that at the very moment you monetise, a lot of your audience instantly turn into trolls. It's like shit magic.

Some trolls don't even realise what or who they are until an ad appears in front of them. Don't worry about them, just be ready for it. In the most part, these people are really boring and expect everything to be given to them for free for the rest of their lives.

And remember, trolls don't want anyone to achieve more than them in life. They want everyone to remain at the same shitty level as them. Don't let them get to you, and if they do, don't let them see it.

39. A SMALL, CONTROLLED BASIS

An audience needs training. This doesn't mean teaching them commands or acting like they aren't all individual people (which is very important btw). You need to gradually drip-feed monetisation methods into your content, so your audience become accustomed to them, are less shocked when they appear and are more likely to act.

This requires finesse. For example, if you want to run ads on your blog's webpages, it's best to go with 2-3 discreetly placed ads to start with, before shifting up to 5-10.

The same goes for other techniques too, even if you have to get in your audience's faces with your chosen monetisation technique, do it as infrequently as possible, and don't repeat anything that will put their attention at risk. This is crucial to your long-term success.

Start small before trying to go big. Don't do anything that will give your audience a nasty shock.

Rushing after money is a common mistake made by creators. By starting small you can test monetisation techniques to discover:

1. How your audience reacts
2. How much you can earn
3. How reliable it is as an income source

Tests mean trying things out on a small, controlled basis. It's easy to get carried away, but it'll break your heart if you lose your audience and have to start all over again.

An awesome winning strategy (that many of the world's most profitable creators use) is to employ a bunch of different monetisation techniques and run them all on a really small scale.

For example, a fashion blog that has high traffic and an engaged audience might:

a) Host a couple of ads on their webpages
b) Do an affiliate deal for a fashion company that they're 'reviewing'
c) Have a funnel that runs from their free content to a paid fashion membership group
d) Run sporadic influencer posts on their social channels.
e) Sell their own merchandise

None of these monetisation techniques will be hit too hard and this way, none of them will kill their audience's attention.

The correct monetisation methods for a content creator are completely dependent on their content type, placement (where it's hosted) and aims, but no matter what you're trying to do, I promise that there's a technique (or combination of them) that will fit your objectives.

40. IT'S A GOOD
EXCUSE TO PARTY

When a creator monetises their content, they look at everything through different coloured glasses. What was an amazing channel for fun and expression, quickly becomes a 'business'.

This is an important point in a creator's development. They must not lose their style or content value, but they also need to think about what's best for their career.

A creator is a business and their content is the product.

It doesn't matter if you're a couple who play pranks on each other, a sports fan writing reviews about your favourite team or an editor who makes compilation videos of extreme weather, you can make serious money when you approach content with the right mindset.

As I mentioned earlier, every time you create a free piece of content, you put a coin into a machine that will one day return your investment. If you're consistent, you'll be able to monetise sooner or later, but it's the decisions you make when you get there that will determine how far you go as a creator. The keyword here: investment.

When you do start earning from your content, don't get over excited. You probably won't earn a lot to start with, this means that it can easily get lost in your regular income (e.g. if you earn an extra £50 a month, it probably won't make a massive difference to your life).

Keep your content earnings separate
from your regular income.

It's easy to get excited when you make a little extra from your content. Some of you might even lose your shit and think it's a good excuse to party (it is btw, just don't spend your content earnings) but it's important that you think about your expenses as the 'business' that you are.

When you earn money from content, you should keep reinvesting that money back into your content channel (and the betterment of your audience) until you earn enough to constantly reinvest money into your content AND make a living from it (on top of that).

Whatever you do, you cannot stop investing in the quality of content. Even if you're making £10,000 a week, you'll need to invest a large chunk of that back into your content to maintain and improve it.

You'll need to buy newer and better equipment (cameras, laptops, mics, software), go to places (travel, accommodation), buy stuff (to review or show your audience), hire more professionals (designers, editors, writers, techies) and always push the boundaries of what can be given away for 'free'.

As well as this, you also need to find space in your

budget to market your content online (and when you start out, that should be your entire budget). Financially backing your content will help you reach more people and capture new members of your audience.

When a creator is starting out, content promotions (social media ads) should be a priority whenever they have the cash to invest.

If I'd just earned my first £100 (all over again), I'd spend the whole wedge on social media ads. I'd split the budget over a few different channels and drip feed the spend on low budgets over a set period (e.g. 7 days). I'd check back every day to see which channel is performing best, then kill the ads that weren't working and push the budget into the one (or two) that's working best. This is easy for me to say because digital marketing is very much my thing (I'll touch on a few strategies for you near the end of this book), but you absolutely must learn how to promote your content.

Great content creators must be great marketers too.

Social ads are actually pretty simple (and incredibly cheap). They appear confusing for novices, but anybody can quickly get the hang of them, and you must.

If you're unsure, look at every other top content creator. They have all reinvested their earnings back into their content, which has improved the quality of their content, increased their audience size and strengthened their earning power. To even think about getting close to them, keep your content income separate from your normal income and reinvest all of it until you have enough left over (after reinvestment) to make a living.

*'The best way to predict your future
is to create it.'*

-ABRAHAM LINCOLN

41. NO WEIRD FISH TOPPING OR ANYTHING LIKE THAT

Every year, an online community celebrate a tradition known as Pizza Day.

BTW: At the time of writing, there have been a total of nine of these days celebrated worldwide.

Pizza Day involves ordering and eating pizza, and although it might sound like a pretty every-day task, it has a very important significance to its (now massive) community.

The tradition was not started by a pizza chef, Italian food lover or cuisine content creator, the annual pizza feast that's celebrated on May 22nd, began because of the now-unforgettable actions of a computer programmer.

Laszlo Hanyecz, the founding father of pizza day, gave birth to the tradition by posting the following topic on a very niche forum[39]:

I'll pay 10,000 bitcoins for a couple of pizzas.. like maybe 2 large ones so I have some left over for the next day. I like having left over pizza to nibble on later. You can make the pizza yourself and bring it to my house or order it for me from a delivery place, but what I'm aiming for is getting food delivered in exchange for bitcoins where I don't have to order or prepare it myself, kind of like ordering a 'breakfast platter' at a hotel or something, they just bring you something to eat and you're happy!

I like things like onions, peppers, sausage, mushrooms, tomatoes, pepperoni, etc.. just standard stuff no weird fish topping or anything like that. I also like regular cheese pizzas which may be cheaper to prepare or otherwise acquire.

If you're interested please let me know and we can work out a deal.

Thanks,
Laszlo

This casual sounding post was the message that would bring about the first ever transaction of a digital currency for a physical product (Bitcoin for pizza).

BTW: I don't own, endorse or trade Bitcoin (I literally have no affiliation with them). The reason I am sharing this story will become very apparent soon.

At the time of posting his message, 10,000 Bitcoins were valued at $41, which would represent a profit for anyone who could buy and deliver the pizzas for cheaper. One responder, by the name of Jercos, did exactly that, trading the coins for two pizzas from Papa Johns.

This sounds pretty normal so far. After all, why wouldn't the cryptocurrency community celebrate the day of their first ever real-world transaction?

This would be the case, if that was the real root of their celebration. Instead of actually commemorating the trade, most people in their community (owners of bitcoin) celebrate Pizza Day because of the growth and increase in value that it represents.

Just 9 years later, those same 10,000 Bitcoins that bought Laszlo two Papa John's Pizzas are now worth approximately $72,510,000[40] (at the time of writing - BitCoin value will fluctuate). That's a currency value increase of 1,768,536x. Pretty good reason to celebrate, right?

This is so relevant to this book because just like a content creator, Laszlo had to put in hard work and effort to mine this many bitcoins. He did it for free, not because anyone was paying him, and he could never have known that his first 10,000 would be worth so much just 9 years later.

BTW: Bitcoin mining is the digital world's version of digging for gold. It's incredibly difficult, requiring high-powered computers, luck and perseverance.

Be prepared, just like Laszlo, to invest your time (and money) in content before trying to earn anything in return. The more you put in, the more you'll be able to take out when the time is right. Just make sure that when you monetise, you don't trade it all for 2 pizzas!

But that story isn't where this section ends. It proves the true value of investing your time into a digital project, but there's room for a little more sauce to add to this point.

Sometime in mid-2013, a Brit named James Howells had a similarly life-changing moment take place because of BitCoin[41].

Howells, like Hanyecz, worked in IT and during Bit-Coin's formative years, mined the currency in his spare time.

After mining approximately 7,500 BitCoin's (starting in 2009). Howells broke his laptop into parts and sold them all on eBay. The only part that he kept was his hard drive, the storage location of this small digital-fortune. Howells put the hard-drive away in a safe location, deciding to wait and see if BitCoin would take off.

Of course, we know today that BitCoin did take off and in today's market his 7,500 haul is worth a whopping $54,382,500...

...but despite this enormous number, Howells still hasn't sold his digital coins. So why hasn't he cashed in?

Hint: He isn't saving it or waiting for it to hit the $100m mark.

Howells accidently threw his hard drive in the bin and it's currently buried below thousands of tonnes of rubbish in Newport, Wales.

During a clear-out, Howells chucked out his old hard drive, now worth upwards of $54 million, and despite his best efforts, has been unable to retrieve it. The IT worker has tried everything to get it back, including assembling investors to fund a landfill dig, but has been blocked in his efforts by Newport Council, who won't give him permission to dig or search on the site (even though he offered them a 10% cut).

If you're into treasure hunting, the Howells hard drive is a real-life story of buried treasure in the 21st century.

The time investment that Howells (and Hanyecz) put into BitCoin was lost years later, because they were careless with the currency. If they had remained consistent and believed in what they were doing, they might be billionaires today (if they had kept mining).

I'm not implying that creating content online will make anyone a billionaire, but if you are going to start, don't cut your journey short or give up, no matter how hard it gets.

42. BE EVERYWHERE ALL THE TIME, JUST DON'T BE THERE TOO MUCH

To earn money online, you first need to give away (a hell of) a lot for free. We've established this as fact and it's been proven (and continues to be) by all the biggest creators, apps and social networks.

You need to be prepared for it and eliminate all fears about working for very little results (to start with). It's the same for everyone.

If you've been paying attention, you might remember that I mentioned 'Instant Gratification' a little while back. Alongside all the free stuff that a content creator needs to give away (in their content), it's this two-word factor that makes a creator's task so difficult, time consuming and riddled with bullshit.

As well as having to give away stuff that once made people millionaires, a content creator must:

- Be where their audience want them to be
- When they want them to be there

- With exactly the education, answers and entertainment that they want
- In the format, medium and length that they demand

Have you ever been shopping and seen one of those annoying kids scream because their parents haven't got them exactly what they wanted?

That red-faced little brat is your audience. They won't shout, scream or scratch if you aren't where they want you to be. They will very rarely throw a tantrum if you aren't in their desired format. They won't tell you they 'hate you' if you don't give them exactly what they want. They'll do something much worse...

...they'll ignore you. And that's the kiss of death for a content creator.

Instant gratification is that spoilt little kid. It's the need for an audience to have what they want, when they want, how they want it, and if you don't give it to them, you're fucked.

Always put your audience's needs ahead of your own.

The internet has caused the need for 'instant gratification' in all of us. Think about your online behaviour and the popularity of websites that are either search engine focussed or include a constantly updating feed of personalised content.

Google and YouTube are the two most visited websites in the world and coincidently, the two most used search engines in the world. Do you think this is a fluke?

Search engines were built to feed our need for instant

gratification. We want instant answers, immediate entertainment and split-second education, and by typing (and now speaking) into a search engine, we can have it.

The same applies to the modern-day content feed that was brought to prominence by social networks like Facebook and Twitter. These feeds are insanely popular (and addictive). When we find a few minutes and have nothing to search for (remember that your dopamine addiction needs nourishing) we log onto social networks and scroll through our content feeds until we find something interesting. This is another clear sign of our need for instant gratification.

As a content creator, I must ensure that I'm where my audience want me, when they want me (which is frighteningly often btw) and how they want me.

Although this might sound difficult, there are a number of ways that a creator can achieve this and as you'd expect, that means more bullshit on our part.

Be everywhere all the time, just don't be there too much.

The first and most obvious tactic is to be absolutely everywhere all the time, but as any content creator will tell you, over-posting will be seen as spammy. As much as you have to be there to gratify your audience's needs, you also can't be there too much (I bet that sounds pretty bull-shitty, right?).

The answer is a frequency that aligns with your industry, audience and content type. This means figuring out a posting schedule and sticking to it at all costs.

A creator should be posting new stuff on social networks every day, even if they're only creating new content once per week (which is the absolute minimum btw). This means breaking big bits of content into smaller pieces and repeating yourself (a lot).

For example, a brand that records a podcast could turn it into a video and post this on one of their days, they could then follow this up with a short video clip of a great stand-alone soundbite from that podcast, then pull a quote and post this as a written piece of content on another day.

This kind of content repetition and repurposing is done by all the big players and as well as achieving your audiences' need for instant gratification, it reduces a creator's workload significantly, allowing us to conquer all social channels.

BTW: When I create a long form piece of content like a blog, it can be used to create months (and months) of good social content for every network.

On top of these repurposing and repetition tactics, a creator can also spy on his competitors and steal their ideas. In most cases, they'll go straight to the brands with the biggest marketing budgets in their industry, find their social profiles and see what, how often and where they're posting new content, and then copy them. These big brands would've invested serious £'s trying to find the best blend for their audience and if that's the same people as yours, stealing and testing their tactics is an awesome place to start.

In a lot of cases, a creator can find a topic that their competitors have proven works and regurgitate the take-aways (like they're an expert) without having any experience or prior knowledge about it. In other words, they act as frauds and gather all the benefits without anybody being able to prove otherwise.

The bullshit rules of content creation demand that if you can't think of enough content topics yourself, just copy somebody else's and pretend that they're yours.

Instant gratification puts shedloads of pressure on a creator to publish high-quality content that always gives away something for free (entertainment or education) as often as possible. And when the weakest of us are put under pressure, we resort to bullshit tactics like repetition, regurgitation, copying and repurposing. This has gone so far that it is now the industry standard.

Many of the world's most popular creators have championed the idea of copying and chopping up content to make it appeal to an audience's need for instant gratification. This means that a content creator must either adhere to these rules to compete or find a way of doing things better.

Instead of us pushing each other to be better, we push each other to be better at bullshitting our audience about how original, creative and knowledgeable we actually are.

Unfortunately, this is one of those cases where the bullshit cannot be beaten. Every creator must be part of this process (until somebody finds a better way to bullshit their audience!). And those creators who are best at this game of smoke, mirrors and instant gratification get quick wins.

This probably sounds like I think I'm above it, but I've been a part of it, especially when I started out. I found big wins in content topics that I knew very little about. In some cases, I'd use Google to find lists e.g. the 5 best... or the 57 most popular... I'd pick a few points from the lists and make my own piece of content (about topics I knew nothing about).

For creators who work with a variety of brands and industries, this type of copying and regurgitation is their bread and butter. And who can blame them? What person knows the everything of everything?

BTW: There are now tons (and tons) of content creation agencies who will create content for any niche, no matter how much they know about the subject. These hired-gun-creators will write an article about dentistry in the morning and a blog about fishing rods at night without a second thought.

Copying and regurgitating is a common tactic for many amateurs, newbs or lazy content creators, who inch their results up at a snail's pace. I was once that newb and have worked in a lot of situations where I've known very little about the industry I was creating in.

Since then, I've realised the true value and pull of original content - stuff that's created from experience and knowledge. And now I can safely say that I'd never go back to replicating. If I don't know enough about a subject, I leave it to somebody else or call in another creator for their expertise.

This tight subject focus has put me in a position where I'm now replicated and referenced. I see competitors copy my topics, headlines and even my content style time after time.

And when others copy you almost every day, I guess it's a pretty good time to write a book, right?

43. ONE OF THESE PHONY RECIPES (PART 1)

I couldn't write an entire book about content creators without shaming some of the biggest bullshiters in the industry.

You've come through a lot of heavy stuff and let's face it, it's been a weird fucking ride up to this point. I don't blame anyone for needing a lay down after some of the sections we've been over. Now it's time for some fun. You deserve it.

The creator types that I'm going to list (in a minute) are alive and kicking in the world of digital and a lot of them are slapping success in the mouth. In fact, some of the top creators have made a living from following one of these phony recipes. The sad thing is that they just don't care. They don't think about you as an audience member, and as long as their tactic pays off, they keep hammering it.

When you think of your audience as an empty bunch of numbers, (sooner or later) they'll become an empty bunch of numbers.

If you ever think about becoming a content creator, it's possible that you'll fall down one of these blackholes at some point in your journey. Whatever happens, just make sure you don't fall in too deep, and you recognise it for what it is (a desperate swipe for glory).

BTW: Some of the points that I've been over in this book will come up now, hopefully this jigs your memory and becomes even clearer.

Let's get into these…

The Ego-Maniacs

This type of creator tells everyone that they're in the content game for other reasons - their brand, their business, their future - when really, they're only in it for their ego.

They have serious ego problems and cannot stand to imagine that they, as amazing and important as they are, can have a social media following of less than 50k.

These people will tell you that they could've been a professional sports person if they wanted, a politician, they could run any business better than the current CEO, they could have written any book, taken any photo, made any design, it's them- and they're special. And if you try to forget this, they're going to remind you on social media, until you are absolutely sure that they really are better than everybody else.

The ego-maniacs are easy to spot because almost all of their sentences include the words 'I', 'me' and 'my'. Their content tends to read/sound a little like this 'I have, I am, I know, I want' and 'about me, without me, with me, because of me' and 'my life, my lessons, my experience, my skills'…

...you get the idea.

Ego maniacs are a common type of content creator. Many of them don't start out that way, but as soon as they get a few likes, their head swells.

They love the sound of their own voice, have a habit of posting way too much content and more than anything, have a massive addiction to social engagement (followers, likes, shares and comments).

The Buyers

Buyers appear to be doing really well; they have tons of followers and always seem to create highly sharable and likeable content. They're quick to tell others about how many followers they have, how many views their most recent video has gained and how big their audience is. Needless to say, it's always in the multiple 4 or 5 figure bracket.

Everything appears amazing on first impression, they're like modern day rockstars, with bags of skill and fans for days...

...but after looking a little closer, you notice that they can't actually play that rock 'n' roll guitar, that they're miming (not singing) and that their crowd of adoring fans are just well-positioned cardboard cut-outs.

Buyers can't be bothered to earn an audience or social engagement through hard-work or creativity, so they pay for it and get trapped in a vicious circle of buying social numbers that they can't escape. These people are more than happy to buy 10k fake followers for the low, low price of £59.99 (although they won't tell a soul about the amazing deal they found).

Ironically, buyers don't have a lot of money. They're usually pretty skint and that's because their earnings are spent trying to prove to the few real people in their audience that they're successful. The rest of their money is spent whenever they publish a post (which is at least once a day) when they pay £9.99 for 1,000 likes.

These accounts have to buy likes, because when they stop, it quickly becomes apparent that almost all of their followers are fake. After all, any account that suddenly loses 1,000's of likes from post to post, is clearly up to something dodgy.

BTW: Lazy buyers are easy to spot, they almost always have 10k-100k followers, but fewer than 50 likes, views and comments on their content.

Although this references the nature of a pure 'buyer', there are tons of creators who dabble in this business. Likes and followers can be bought by subscription, constantly topping up real numbers with tons of fakes. And as we've already uncovered (a little earlier) these 'buyers' are absolutely everywhere.

The Spammers

We all know that one person who shows up at every social event, even though he pisses everyone off, right? The spammer is the digital world's version of that guy - on crack.

Spammers make their gains by being absolutely everywhere. They make request after request, in the hope that someone will be stupid enough to accept. They send private messages, leave comments, fire out emails and make friend requests...

...but something doesn't seem quite right about their requests. They just have that (insert word here) feeling to them. We've all had them, including (insert name here), especially when we've worked for a brand like (insert business name here).

There is no possible way that a spammer could write and send that many unique messages, so instead of this, they send out 1,000's of the shittest generic communications you're ever likely to see.

I receive 40-80 emails and direct messages (particularly on LinkedIn) like this every single day. At first I ignore them, but if I notice generic messages from the same name appear twice, I chuck them straight in the spam folder (or block them).

Template messages always seem to start with a very broad compliment before following it up with some sort of request (usually asking me to do something to help them). I guess spammers think we're blinded by flattery. Here are a few examples of the type of universal praise I'm talking about:

BTW: These are all real message intros that I've received from people today (when I say 'today' I mean the time of writing)

'I surfed the net and then, I came across your fantastic website with beneficial and informative posts'

'I checked out your website and found it to be a splendid place to read and share.'

'I've been following your blog for a while, and have found a few of them very interesting and useful. I appreciate your excellent content writing. Thanks for providing great content on your website.'

I could fill an entire book with a week's worth of generic emails, either that, or open up my LinkedIn inbox and use the 8,000,000 generic messages in there.

You get the picture - spammers send out the same message to tons of people across a range of platforms, hoping that somebody will do something for them. This request might be a simple follow, post like, link exchange, email list promotion, social share…the possibilities are endless.

Whenever I'm reading emails, considering messages and potential collaboration requests, I always look for the human element first.

If somebody genuinely wants to work with me they'll write a real message (it only takes 10 minutes). And likewise, when I send out messages or requests, I always try to personalise and tailor them for the recipient, I'd rather spend 10 minutes writing something to a specific person, than 10 minutes collecting emails for a generic email blast.

The No Messagers

I'm still not sure whether the 'no messagers' create content because they're bored or because they genuinely believe that strangers want to know who they are. Whatever the reason, I'd prefer it if they did it away from me.

'No messagers' are people who literally have no plan,

topic or idea in their content. Nothing they do has direction or meaning, and every other piece of content pulls their digital presence in a different direction. In one post they're on video talking about politics, in the next they're talking about their pets, and in the one after that they're preaching about how you should live your life.

These accounts are basically private profiles on steroids. This wouldn't be a bad thing if the account's owners weren't completely delusional. They believe that the whole world should want to see posts and videos about their life when they have no message or personal connection with their prospective audience.

The no messagers are basically wannabe celebrities, without skill, talent or quality in their content. They're arrogant, without having any reason to feel that way.

Content must have some sort of meaning. Even if you are creating a personal brand or trying to become an influencer, you need to have a consistent message and corner of the market that you're trying to pin down (e.g. fitness, fashion, pets, design). A skill or specialism gives people a reason to follow an account and shows an audience what to expect.

The Serial Repeaters

Following this type of content creator is like watching a hamster that was running on a wheel but has now lost control and is clinging on for dear life, doing loop after loop after loop.

A serial repeater is a creator who repeats the same thing over and over again. They repeat the same messages, use the same camera angles, write about the same topic, record with the same backgrounds…you get the idea.

They are a stark contrast to the 'no messagers', as they only have one message and they hammer it repeatedly. This sounds like a strong strategy, but their message is so specific that it soon bores and irritates their audience.

Serial repeaters don't start out their content creating careers like this. Instead, they're beaten to near death by the very real (and raw) existence of being a creator, lose their passion for content and lack the motivation to improve themselves.

I feel sorry for serial repeaters and fear that it's a sign of the beginning of the end for anybody working in the digital space. It symbolises fatigue, lack of care and interest, content burnout and a rudderless strategy.

Everything a creator does should have purpose and must complement other pieces of content. If you ever feel like you're falling into the trap of serial repetition, step away from your content and try to reconnect with the reasons you started (hopefully that's a passion for your content's topic and subject).

44. ONE OF THESE PHONY RECIPES (PART 2)

The Perfect Life(rs)

They wake up looking beautiful, are forever residing besides infinity pools, only fly in private jets, are never sad or down, only wear designer clothes and always date the ideal member of the opposite sex, and they aren't done there. They holiday on super-yachts, live in mansions, have the cutest pets, can eat incredibly decadent food without it affecting their figures, have perfected their bodily functions so they never need the toilet...

...these motherfuckers are perfect. Their life, holidays, houses, cars, clothes and of course - them, are nothing short of flawless. They have it all and they want you to know it.

The only odd thing about 'perfect life(rs)' is that they tend to disappear in their late 20's/early 30's. I'm not sure if they regenerate or suddenly come to their senses, but whatever it is, they very rarely make it past this age (on social) - perhaps they never age.

The perfect life(rs) have a preferred platform - Instagram – and their life revolves around the beauty and impossible excellence of their Insta profile.

This all sounds amazing, but this type of creator actually lives under a very real threat - other perfect life(rs).

Occasionally, somebody else on Instagram appears to have a more perfect life than this type of creator. This is a disaster and a perfect lifer must retaliate. In order for them to get one over on their competitor, they have no choice but to go to the exact same location and take the exact same shot - with the aim of theirs being a teeny-weeny bit better (this is usually achieved by editing or using a new filter).

Perfect lifers tend to come from fortunate backgrounds and are able to do things in the early stages of their adult life that others must fight their entire adult life to earn. The success of their parents (or grandparents) is no fault of their own, but their addiction with rubbing it in the face of the rest of the world is a little unnecessary.

I have never been in this position, but from what I've seen of perfect lifers (from first-hand experience) a lot of their happiness is faked and they're actually incredibly insecure and completely obsessed with the approval of others. I can't speak with knowledge of all perfect lifer type creators, but just remember that there's much more going on behind their photos than they want you to see.

It's my opinion that the authentic will always outlast the fake, the real will always triumph over the forged, and the relatable will invariably beat the distant. But maybe I'm just bitter because I haven't been in 6,465 infinity pools...

The Don't Practice What They Preachers

If I told you that 30 minutes of meditation every morning will make you a much happier person, you'd expect me to know that from personal experience, right? You'd assume that these teachings were based on my own practice, wouldn't you?

The world of content is packed with creators who don't practice what they preach. They tell you to meditate every day, but they don't do it themselves, they tell you to wake up at a certain time every day, but they get up two hours later, they tell you that you need to follow their specific tactics and strategies to become a millionaire, when they aren't even millionaires themselves.

This type of content creator is rife and although many of them are incredibly easy to spot, they're getting better at hiding.

The core of their content is always copied or replicated from other creators (who are authentic experts in their industry). They don't know what they're preaching, they very rarely understand the ins and outs of their subject and they have never worked a day in the industry they preach to others about.

If you're ever unsure about a creator's history or expertise, ask them about their experience. Would somebody who is genuine have something to hide?

The Comfort Zoners

Pushing back the boundaries of what's comfortable is a very real part of a content creator's day job.

The only way to grow and improve your content is to push yourself out of your comfort zone. As a creator, it's easy to become trapped by your own work and style, but at some point, you must recognise that this will only restrict your success.

Be brave!

The internet is full of creators who have spent a long time building up their profile, web presence and audience, only to plateau for the rest of their careers. This is because they've never been brave enough to break out of their comfort zone.

If a content idea scares you, it's definitely a good idea. Don't hesitate when you think of something that intimidates you. Keep pushing your boundaries and you'll achieve the rewards you deserve.

The Throw Money At It-ers

Have no patience and more money than sense? If that sounds like you, you'd fit nicely into this group of content creators.

These people simply cannot be bothered to start from scratch, so they chuck cash at every strategy in the book. They buy influencer mentions, pay for collaborations and ads, run promotions on other channels, they'd even pay your mother if she agreed to hold a sandwich board outside your local kebab shop.

Throwing cash at your content definitely has the desired effect. If you pay companies to show your content to more people, that's what's going to happen. However, this comes with one significant drawback, particularly for new accounts:

If all you ever do is back your content with a pile

of cash, how do you know if it's any good?

Even average content will gain likes and follows online if it's shown to enough people.

I have always believed that backing content with cash is an amazing strategy, but I know that when creators do this they must occasionally lower their spend to see the true value of their content. If people are only liking and following my stuff because I'm paying a social network to get those results, it says a lot about my work.

The formative stages of a creator's journey are the best times to learn what an audience likes. Trust me, the difference between a piece of content that gets 5 likes and one that gets 12 is a lot bigger than just 7 likes, especially when you're starting out.

If you really want to succeed at content creation, discover what content is most worthy of your cash before investing it.

The Regurgitators

What happens when somebody has:

- No experience
- No knowledge
- No skills
- No creativity
- No pride
- No care
- 100% delusion
- 1000% desire to become famous (for no reason)

Any ideas?

In the world of content creation somebody like this will find a host (or several) and consistently regurgitate their content. This means copying their messages, their format, their style, their clothes, their language, their breathing speed, their hair products, their button colours...you get the idea.

Regurgitators are either a) completely obsessed with the creator that they're copying - so much so that they literally want to be them, or b) completely obsessed with becoming rich and powerful because they're insanely insecure.

There is nothing unique or valuable about a regurgitator's content. It's like eating your dinner and then bringing it all back up and eating it again. Which version would you prefer, the first (the original) or the sicked up rendition (the regurgitated).

The content world is jam-packed with creator's like this, and while I take my hat off to people for trying, I feel sorry for them for hiding behind other creator's messages. If you have a personality (which everyone does btw) and some sort of experience (which everyone also does) you have a message to share.

Don't hide behind others, stand up beside them.

Regurgitation is the easiest form of content to create. It demands very little, but it also does very little. It doesn't separate a creator (because tons of other regurgitators are doing it too), it won't show people who you (or your brand) are, it doesn't highlight what you're best at and basically tells the world that you don't have any ideas of your own.

45. YOU'RE GOING TO HAVE TO SUCK UP A HELLUVA LOT

Being a creator isn't as glamorous as you (probably) first thought. It's one of the grittiest, toughest and most competitive professions out there - and these negative factors are only going to get more extreme (as the bullshit takes a tighter stranglehold over the biggest content platforms).

Every time a creator posts a photo of themselves on an idyllic beach, or a blogger publishes a post about all the amazing benefits they've gained, or a YouTuber releases a video of themselves reviewing tons of free products, it inspires the next generation to dream of the same 'amazing life'.

If this book has taught you anything, it's that not everything is quite as it seems. The real life of a content creator is very different to what you might expect, and if the next generation of creators are going to succeed (and actually be happy) it's important that they understand what it takes to 'make it'.

Having tons of ideas and bags of creativity is all well and good but sadly, it isn't enough on its own. There are 3 specific skills that every creator must have if they are going to make it in today's digital world without quitting or cheating (and inevitably being caught out).

The first is an antifragility that is unwavering in the face of adversity, pain and the inevitable bullshit that content is going to throw at you. As a creator you're going to face trolls, compete against bullshitters and (occasionally) put in tons of work (aka time and money) for very little results.

As a creator, you're going to have to suck up a helluva lot.

A creator has to become stronger through adversity. All those who've made it have done the same. It's proven to be a decisive characteristic in separating the serious creators from the fakers.

BTW: Stephen King had his first novel rejected 30 times before it was accepted for publishing. Vincent Van Gogh sold one painting in his entire lifetime. Albert Einstein couldn't speak until he was 4 years old. Steven Spielberg was rejected twice by the University of Southern California's School of Cinematic Arts. James Dyson created 5,126 failed prototypes (over the course of 15 years) before creating his best-selling vacuum cleaner.

Learning to look into the face of negativity, hate and definitive rejection without a muscle twitching (and even enjoying it) is an incredible trait to have. Where others seek approval and the comfort of their 'safety zone', a creator looks for rejection so they can better understand how far their limitations are (and become stronger because of them).

When you know where your limits lie,
seek them and push them back.

By being (or learning) antifragility, you can achieve so much more in all areas of your life, not just content creation.

Failure in itself is an accomplishment, relish
it when it comes around.

BTW: The first people to remind you of your failure are those who have never been brave enough to give it a shot themselves. When you hear negativity from these people, use it as reassurance that you're doing the right thing and that you're learning a strength that they could never achieve.

However, this is easy for me to say. I'm passed the point of negativity affecting me. I'm bulletproof to it (with regards to content) and hate or love my stuff, I'm going to keep publishing it (for myself and businesses online).

Reaching this zen-like-level of apathy isn't easily won - but by having the second trait in my 3 must-haves, a creator gives themselves a much better chance...

46. BUT CAN THEY DO IT ON A RAINY TUESDAY NIGHT IN STOKE?

People perform when they care. When they don't give a shit, they put in minimal effort (this is old news for people in leadership positions).

Many failed creators can handle a lot of the bullshit factors I've covered in this book. They can deal with the negativity, the cheats, the lies, the online smokescreens, but there's one thing that they are not able to do: get themselves to care.

People tell themselves that they care, they tell others and make all the right noises, but when it comes to actually showing it, they take long breaks, procrastinate, watch cat videos online, touch themselves, eat chocolate, find excuses, go to events and neglect their plans.

In other words, they do everything they can to show that they don't care.

BTW: Caring isn't a creator's must-have trait, it's a prerequisite for anybody in any job. If you don't care, you're going to plod along in the average bracket for the rest of your life.

For people who work for others, most of their 'care' comes from the extrinsic (external factors) - usually in the form of money.

For instance, do you think that sales guy wants to cold call people all day, or is it the commission that's driving him? Do you think that woman at McDonalds is working hard because she loves burgers, or is she trying to get a promotion so she can earn a decent living? Do you think the binman really loves trash, or is it the security of his salary that's driving him?

This is how the 'employed' are motivated to care (or not care at all) about the profession that they find themselves in.

A truly committed creator who is prepared to drive their online presence through thick and thin, deal with all the shit that's thrown at them and wade through the digital world's mounds of content bullshit, cannot be motivated by the extrinsic.

Creators must have intrinsic motivation (forces from their internal psyche) for their care, and this leads us to our second must-have, passion.

Passion is a word that is bashed around far too loosely. It has become some broad meaning catchphrase that people in every profession use to describe their ideal 'team member', "above all else, they have to be passionate."

The word has been so overused that many people don't

even understand what it means anymore. For most, it has even become manufacturable. Instead of just 'acting busy', people also 'act passionately' when the right people are watching or something they hold dear is on the line (usually a pay rise).

For me, passion means something else, something very specific. And it goes hand-in-hand with pressure.

Pressure is often mistaken as a negative force. It brings about images of a red-faced person, sweating, squinting, wiping their brow, performing under strain. This isn't the type of pressure that somebody who is passionate finds themselves in.

Pressure is a privilege.

Passion drives a pressure that very few are lucky enough to feel. Only those destined for the top are fortunate enough to understand this.

I'm a football fan (soccer to the yanks reading this) and in England we have a saying about football players:

They look great and might have all the skill in the world, but can they do it on a rainy Tuesday night in Stoke?

BTW: Stoke City FC have a reputation as a very physical team, who were once known for kicking other teams off the park and making themselves incredibly hard to beat. No nonsense, at its most primitive.

My 'rainy Tuesday night in Stoke' is a regular Thursday morning at home or in the office. It's a time when there is no external pressure, when all the targets are being hit, when there's a ton of awesome content ready to go, when the audience are chatting to you, when the stats are all reading positive. You can see the difference in those who are passionate when the going is good and everything is running on time, in perfect order.

Anybody can feel pressure when there's a fast-approaching deadline, when employees, bosses, partners, friends, children or bank balances are making demands. That's their fault. That's the squeeze they've put themselves in and let's be clear - it's a pressure created from an external force - not themselves or their desire to be better at what they do.

Real pressure is a privilege that very few creators are blessed enough to experience and it comes from a passion in one of two places:

1. Passion for their topic (e.g. nature, environment, sport, gaming, fitness, business)
2. Passion for their medium (e.g. video, writing, audio, photography, illustration, painting, drawing, music, etc.)

When a creator has intrinsic passion derived from either (or both) of these factors, their ability to succeed is only limited by how well they can deal with all the other bullshit factors in this book.

A creator who is motivated because they love to write, will always aim to write better, a videographer will always strive to produce better video content because they fucking love the medium, a huge sports fan will not stop reporting on sport or let their levels drop just because they posted a well-received article, a creator who is passionate about the environment will not sit around all afternoon watching YouTube videos or playing mobile games because a few extra people liked their latest content.

Passion gives a creator an edge and there are just too many passionate people in the world (with access to a digital channel) for you to fake it and compete.

47. WINNING IS RELATIVE

The final content creator must-have goes against 90% of the junk (that I've brought to your attention) in this book. In a world where transparency has never been more important, being authentic means (almost) everything.

Be real.

If you have to think hard about how you're acting, what you're saying, how you're working, your mannerisms, your accent, your use of language, it means that you're trying to be somebody you aren't.

We're all sick of fakers, liars and manipulators. They're ten-a-penny online, so why join them?

There is an audience out there for everyone.

Whoever you are and whatever you know, there is a group of people who want to hear from you. There is a collective out there who are desperate to discover more quality content about even the tiniest of niches.

BTW: In some cases, becoming 'internet famous' (in an industry) means gaining just 1,000 followers, to others, it means 100k+. The point is that it really doesn't matter, as long as you stay true to yourself, what you know and who you really are. I know creators who are super famous in very specific niches and have followings that relfect this. In the eyes of their followers, they're up there with the most important people in their lives.

'Winning' is relative.

You cannot be someone that you aren't, but by being true to yourself, you give yourself the best shot at achieving your real potential as a content creator. Do not mimic, act or lie because you'll have to do that forever. Speak in your own voice, do it at your speed, with your knowledge and in a way that makes you happy.

Faking it is the easiest (and most cowardly) thing you can do. Being yourself takes balls. It means opening yourself up to anyone who's interested, it means showing the world that you're truly happy with who you are and what you can do.

You (and the things you know) are awesome - don't ever lose sight of that.

48. OUTSIDE A TOYS 'R' US IN THE EARLY HOURS OF THE MORNING

I remember being a child, when the only computers we had at school were made by Acorn. It was in these formative years that VHS players, CD's and digital wristwatches were highly desired pieces of tech.

I remember trading huge Nintendo game cartridges at school and being amazed by the technology inside a *Tamagotchi* (my Mum queued up outside a *Toys 'R' Us* in the early hours of the morning to get me that thing - thanks Mum).

And whilst these gadgets sound ancient, they aren't. I'm 31 years old and have grown from child to man at the same time as the internet. The digital world is young and it's our responsibility to help it develop into a force for good - not negativity, lies, hatred, discrimination, fear or bullshit.

The internet is an amazing place and it's our job
to leave it in a better state than we found it.

Nobody has a bigger impact on the digital world than a content creator. These are the people who dictate trends, direct followers, create movements, influence audiences and share the content that can change lives.

Let's stop trying to fuck each other over and use the internet to make the real world a better place.

The internet deserves better. People are entitled to more (and they're starting to realise it). Be a force for everything genuine. It's the only way to win from here on out.

BONUSES

What kind of creator would I be if I didn't offer you something extra?

I want to give all readers the opportunity to get a free first look at any of my upcoming books and high-value content (e.g. video, audio, blogs). This will act as a queue-jumping ticket that skips ahead of publish dates and website pre-orders.

If you want to get a FREE copy of an upcoming title, receive content ahead of everyone else, share your opinion with me and stay ahead of everyone else in the content world (whilst having a good time along the way) you should subscribe here:

SUBSCRIBE HERE->www.joshbarney.blog/newsletter

BTW: I'm working on an amazingly high-value title right now (that I'm really excited to share with you!).

And make sure you're following me on social:

Twitter: *@joshbarneyblog*

Facebook: *@joshbarneyb*

NOTES FROM THE AUTHOR

What did you think of the book? Any good?

One of the most influential factors on our behaviour and those of the people closest to us, are personal recommendations.

If you have any thoughts on this book, please leave a review (on the site that you purchased it from) to benefit others who are in a similar position to you.

I've spent hours/days/weeks/months creating this for you, please take two minutes of your time to return the favour.

Before I sign off and leave this thing to the (yawn) *Appendix,* I'd like to thank you for taking the time to make it this far. It's been a privilege having you around for so long.

Good luck with your content journey and if there's anything I can help with, don't be afraid to hit me up. I try to give free advice to anybody who is smart enough to find my email address (and patient enough to wait for a reply).

Thank you, you're awesome!

NOTES/RESOURCES

1:
https://www.statista.com/statistics/617136/digital-population-worldwide/

2:
https://www.worldometers.info/world-population/population-by-country/

3:
www.statisticbrain.com (Statistic Brain Research Institute)

4:
https://www.cnbc.com/2016/12/30/read-all-about-it-the-biggest-fake-news-stories-of-2016.html Hannah Ritchie, 30/12/2016

5:
https://www.statista.com/chart/17518/internet-use-one-minute/, 29/03/2019, (Statista)

6:
oneredpaperclip.blogspot.com, Kyle MacDonald

7:
Based on the $100 per 10k follower rule: https://later.com/blog/instagram-influencers-costs/, Lexie Car-

bone, 10/04/2019

8:
https://www.harpersbazaar.com/uk/celebrities/news/a28695143/celebrities-most-fake-instagram-followers/ , Jessica Davis, 04/07/2019

9:
https://www.prweek.com/article/1593685/taylor-swift-kardashians-neymar-among-celebs-fake-followers-finds-new-study

10:
https://www.icmp.ac.uk/fake-followers/, Institute of Contemporary Music Performance

11:
http://www.milliondollarhomepage.com/, Alex Tew

12:
http://lifefaker.com/, Sanctus.io

13:
https://www.hbo.com/chernobyl, HBO

14:
https://www.fakeavacation.com/

15:
https://www.dailymail.co.uk/femail/article-6435173/People-taking-Instagram-photos-inside-fake-private-jet-interior-inside-store.html, Robyn Turk, 29/11/2018

16:
https://kotaku.com/in-japan-you-can-hire-fake-friends-for-facebook-and-in-1802517318

17:
https://selfiefactory.co.uk/

18:
https://www.instagram.com/lilmiquela/?hl=en   +
https://www.thecut.com/2018/05/lil-miquela-digital-
avatar-instagram-influencer.html,   Emilia   Petrarca,
14/05/2018

19:
https://www.rejectiontherapy.com/, Jia Jiang

20:
Taleb, Nassim Nicholas. *Antifragile*, November 2012

21:
https://twitter.com/tescomobile

22:
https://twitter.com/Wendys

23:
https://www.independent.co.uk/news/uk/home-
news/teenage-suicides-england-and-wales-2010-ons-
a8522331.html,   The   Independent,   Shebab   Khan,
04/09/2018

24:
https://www.rsph.org.uk/our-work/campaigns/status-
of-mind.html, Royal Society for Public Health,

25:
https://www.psychologytoday.com/gb/basics/
dopamine

26:

https://www.ncbi.nlm.nih.gov/pmc/articles/
PMC2824994/

27:
https://www.ncbi.nlm.nih.gov/pmc/articles/
PMC3932907/

28:
https://www.drugabuse.gov/publications/drugs-
brains-behavior-science-addiction/drugs-brain

29:
Olds, J., & Milner, P. (1954). Positive reinforce-
ment produced by electrical stimulation of septal area
and other regions of rat brain. *Journal of Compara-
tive and Physiological Psychology, 47*(6), 419–427. https://
doi.org/10.1037/h0058775

30:
http://sitn.hms.harvard.edu/flash/2018/dopamine-
smartphones-battle-time/, 01/05/2018

31:
https://www.drugwise.org.uk/how-much-crime-is-
drug-related/

32:
https://www.forbes.com/sites/
erikkain/2014/02/11/10-things-you-may-not-know-
about-flappy-bird/

33:
https://mashable.com/2014/02/10/flappy-bird-
story/?europe=true

34:

https://mashable.com/2014/02/04/flappy-bird-developer/?europe=true, Mashable, 04/02/2014

35:
https://www.vam.ac.uk/blog/news/the-rise-and-fall-of-flappy-bird-and-the-collecting-of-the-vas-first-app

36:
https://kotaku.com/flappy-bird-is-making-50-000-a-day-off-ripped-art-1517498140

37:
https://www.vice.com/en_us/article/d738n7/flappy-bird-phones-are-seeing-bids-of-90000-on-ebay

38:
https://blog.rescuetime.com/screen-time-stats-2018/, RescueTime, 21/03/2019

39:
https://bitcointalk.org/index.php?topic=137.0, 18/05/2010

40:
https://www.coindesk.com/price/bitcoin

41:
https://www.independent.co.uk/life-style/gadgets-and-tech/news/bitcoin-value-james-howells-newport-landfill-hard-drive-campbell-simpson-laszlo-hanyecz-a8091371.html, Ther Independent, Aatif Sulleyman, 04/12/2017

ABOUT THE AUTHOR

Josh Barney is an award-winning content marketer and a director and shareholder of Einstein Marketer - an awesome marketing agency specialising in social media, ad buying and marketing strategy.

In 2019, Josh won the UK Blog Awards for the Einstein Marketer agency blog, as well as being nominated for Content Creator of the Year, Marketing Blog of the Year and helping the agency gain a nomination for Social Media Marketing Agency of the Year for client and in-house work, at national and international award shows.

Since Einstein Marketer started up at the end of 2017, Josh's work has helped the agency grow from 0 to ~100k followers, increase organic traffic by more than 10x from 2018 to 2019, generate 2000+ leads per month (not including client work) and grow as a business in terms of team size, digital footprint and revenue.

He has previously worked as a blogger, content manager and freelance writer, but now spends most of his time creating and directing content for Einstein Marketer, as well as his own personal blog and video content (www. joshbarney.blog).

Printed in Great Britain
by Amazon